The Respectful Manager

Many people are confused by mixed messages from their managers. About 85% of the pool of managers are malevolent, who do not care about the organisation and use the structure for their own needs of power and control. We know what a good manager looks like, but in complex social interactions within organisations this can be confused with the manipulations of the malevolent managers, from CEO to the lowest grade supervisor.

The Respectful Manager: The Guide to Successful Management is about the application of the Executive Impression Management type of the Respectful Manager, derived from new ground-breaking research regarding fraudster managers. It explains clearly and precisely what a good manager looks like and behaves like with their co-workers. In this book, the foundations are laid to understand and recognise a Respectful Manager. This is critical for management training purposes and for managerial recruitment and promotion procedures. For those looking at increasing profitability, increasing competitive edge, and engaging their workforce in fulfilling work, the Respectful Manager is the key.

This book is a must read for those who aspire to management roles, including senior management, as a guide to the very best practice in the field.

Terry A. Sheridan is a Fellow of the Australian Institute of Management and a Fellow of the Institute of Leadership and Management (UK), a member of the Fraud Advisory Panel (UK) and an Affiliate Member of the Council of International Investigators. She is also the Managing Director of Guardian Angel Holdings Pty Ltd, Australia.

The Respectful Manager
The Guide to Successful Management

Terry A. Sheridan

Routledge
Taylor & Francis Group

LONDON AND NEW YORK

First published 2019 by Routledge

2 Park Square, Milton Park, Abingdon, Oxon, OX14 4RN

605 Third Avenue, New York, NY 10017

Routledge is an imprint of the Taylor & Francis Group, an informa business

First issued in paperback 2020

British Library Cataloguing in Publication Data
A catalogue record for this book is available from the British Library

Library of Congress Cataloging-in-Publication Data
Names: Sheridan, Terry A., author.
Title: The respectful manager : the guide to successful management / Terry Sheridan.
Description: First Edition. | New York : Routledge, [2019] | Includes bibliographical references and index.
Identifiers: LCCN 2018034983| ISBN 9781138306677 (hardback) | ISBN 9781315141916 (ebook)
Subjects: LCSH: Management. | Leadership. | Organizational change.
Classification: LCC HD31.2 .S44 2019 | DDC 658--dc23
LC record available at https://lccn.loc.gov/2018034983

ISBN: 978-1-138-30667-7 (hbk)
ISBN: 978-0-367-78764-6 (pbk)

Typeset in Times New Roman
by Taylor & Francis Books

To my mother in law, Mary Westall, Chevalier (Knight), Legion D'Honneur. One of the most courageous women I know.

Contents

Illustrations

Preface

I would like to thank all of those people who have supported me in this endeavour.

It all began in 2016 with an idea from Paula Higgs – 'Well, what *is* Respectful Management?' – that started me on the journey of writing this book. I am very grateful for her thought provoking question, as with my head stuck in the data to me it was obvious, but it started to become difficult to explain to others. Not because of lack of theory, but because to write a normative book on the ideal type of management is fraught with the danger of becoming a boring list. However, she was quite right, it needed to be explained within the context of Executive Impression Management to compare and contrast with the more prevalent malevolent managers that are described in my innovative research.

Kristina Abbotts, Commissioning Editor at Taylor & Francis, saw the merit too of this information having to be out there, and pushed for its acceptance as well as my referees who knew my work. Being a completely independent researcher and practitioner with no university or institutional backing, I did not have an army of postgrad students to continue the research beyond my doctoral study. Once again, I had to sit down and write it myself, which is always an enjoyable experience if only life did not get in the way!

This time my writing was based in Brittany, France and not Indonesia as before. I still share my time with Australia and Indonesia, but for strategic reasons concerning my business, being on Europe's doorstep was a better option. However, there have been times when I have been wrapped up in woollens and blankets to overcome the cold, huddling my laptop to keep warm. How I missed the tropical warmth of Bali and the heat of summer in Perth, Australia! But it has all been worth it, and again, I am very thankful that I didn't have to write this in a shed at the bottom of the garden.

I must thank my family and friends for their constant support, as well as health practitioners, who have got me through the writing of the book. My husband John Westall is a tower of support and strength to me, always encouraging me and doing the background work of house and dog duties as well as looking after his own business.

It remains, though, at my own doorstep if there are any errors in this book. But the theory is solid and I agree with Paula, it is time to get the information out there about what is good management, to combat the facile, ill-informed and trite commentary that we get in the media. If managers modelled their behaviour on Respectful Management, the world indeed will be a far better place.

Uzel Près L'Oust
Brittany
France
2018

First aid

There will be people looking at this book as they are suffering from the effects of bad management. Most notably these effects will be in the form of bullying, physical or emotional and feel bad about themselves, perhaps blaming themselves for attracting or standing up to a manager and felt the full brunt of his or her malevolent overt or covert behaviour.

I want to reassure you that what you are feeling is similar to many if not thousands of employees around the world and feel pushed to thoughts of ending the pain through self-harm.

What you must do is talk to someone about what is happening to you, and if it is thoughts of ending it all, then contact The Samaritans immediately. They have toll-free numbers in practically every country and are easily found on the internet. The Samaritans are trained people who totally understand what you are going through. They won't stop you and call the police and so on if you wish to go ahead, but 9 times out of ten you will feel better and see a way through the pain that you are experiencing. In fact, on their website they say: 'People talk to us anytime they like, in their own way - about whatever's getting to them. You don't have to be suicidal.'

If you are a co-worker of someone who is experiencing a lot of emotional pain at work, then do not hesitate to encourage that person to get help. One helpful hand may stop a tragedy beyond compare to their family and friends.

If you are in human resources and see such a person, you have a duty of care to do something to help the individual concerned. If you are a manager, the same responsibility applies to you. Do not engage in judgement or blame, the individual needs help and you must alleviate it in any way possible immediately.

The best band-aid

As suicides for women are increasing (Samaritans 2018), one note from a national research study I undertook on women manager's unemployment is particularly appropriate (Sheridan, 2005). The women felt that they had no one to reach out to, as their circle of friends and family were limited in the way that they could understand their work situation. Developing 'buddy groups' or networks can go a long way for a professional woman to get the understanding and support that she needs when the chips are down.

1   Introduction to the code of Executive Impression Management

Good management. What is it? How do we achieve it? People seem to know it when they see it but ask them directly and they are lost for words and at best shrug their shoulders. I know this, as I have tried. It is seemingly intangible, a nice glowing feeling that you get when you work with a manager that you like. There is a great deal of information about what a good manager is, including top ten lists ad nauseam, some compiled by fairly good sources too. But it still is a melange of what constitutes good management. Authors contradict others, the media pick up the latest research and then drop it when another study comes along. Information about good management is about as confusing as looking up what is a good diet these days. One theme that is apparent is that there is no cohesive collection of thought.

So why have I written a book about it? Well, that is because I accidentally found what good managerial behaviour is through a doctoral research study concerning managerial fraud. It is the first time that good management has had a strong grounding in a theory which is satisfactory, compared to what has been offered by scholars and practitioners. I found that there was a strong contingent of managers who lie to their co-workers and pretend to be good managers, whereas in reality they are not. Once you take the bad managers out of the equation, only good managers remain, and that is what I found, but they all share common characteristics. There will be probably some bad managers reading this who will take on the latest ideas and apply them in their workplace so that they can deceive you. I can assure you that their attempts will fail once you understand the theory behind this book. I go into some detail for that very reason. A bogus manager just cannot keep wearing the mask of a good manager for long, and once you are aware of what to look for, you will be well armed against deception.

But it does beg the question: why do managers go to such lengths to deceive others? If they are not defrauding the company, when it is understandable that they wouldn't want others to latch on to what they are doing, why would they do so? Managers are not spies, who have to live a dangerous life in order to survive to carry on with their deceit, motivated perhaps by ideology or money or a coveted citizen status. They are ordinary human beings who have desired the position or have been thrust into it, without having a clue to what to do.

I think a lot of this behaviour that we see is down to the fact that they do not want others to see them as they really are. Hence the need for status to show others who they aspire to be. Company cars, large bonuses, sometimes housing or lower interest rates for loans and mortgages are all factors which reward this deceitful behaviour. Perhaps this is accidental in the system design, but anyone can get into prestigious positions if they lie enough. We have seen this with doctors operating without licences; CEOs who have been exposed on their credentials, or rather, lack thereof; pilots who pretend they have been to flying school when they have not; presidents and members of parliament who lie about their expenditures to deceive their electorates. The rewards are big enough for many people to want to deceive.

But there is something fundamentally missing from this activity, and that is that the rewards are not transferable to the after-life if you believe in that, and if you do not, then you know that it is impossible to fill your tomb with riches like the Pharaohs, because you really can't take it with you. No, there is something logically wrong with that status-seeking way of life. There is no consideration about leaving their footprints in the sand. Have they done any good on this planet, did they help anyone? Did they look after their families and children or their community? Unfortunately, all that activity in order to receive consumer goods is wrong when the organisation is used for their own needs and gain. Call me an idealist, I really do not mind, but is that what life is all about? Whoever dies with the most toys wins? I am asking such questions because the malevolent managers that my Executive Impression Management theory describes do not think in the long term: with them it's here and now, with a five-year plan at best. It's all about getting to the top.

When you look at organisations there is disturbing activity going on; employees talk about bullying, constructive dismissals, sexist behaviour, exploitation at its worst, all at the hands of managers. So, if they win all the toys, then why, it must be asked, do they abuse people and allow this sort of behaviour to continue? Is having lots of status symbols and living in grand mansions not enough? No, there is something more deeply disturbing at work here. Rampant consumerism is only a symptom; there are more awful behaviours that are happening.

It seems that we almost expect organisations to be hideous, and finding one that is not is like a breath of fresh air. They are certainly not the norm. Most people put up with managerial shenanigans and try to get on with their life, even though work becomes a stressful experience. Sleep is affected, family relationships become disrupted, friends become distant. Over a length of time stress kicks in with a lowered immune response, which leads to long term illness and early death. It is a fact that men die earlier than women; it has been explained in part by the protective influence of oestrogen, but there may very well be a different explanation. Women tend not to be in the workforce as long as their male counterparts, due to child rearing, aged parental care and other factors. This leads to part-time and casual work, so their participation in a workplace tends to be lower over their lifespan.

Certainly, we know that stress for males and females can lead to smoking and excessive drinking of alcohol, and these two factors alone are definitely linked to cancers and heart disease. There are many possibilities, but none have looked thoroughly at the effect of work on lifespan, apart from the famous Whitehall studies on British civil servants, where they found that the lower the grade of worker, the shorter the lifespan (Marmot et al., 1978). This could be partly due to bullying as it is now recognised, but this was not a factor considered in the first study.

Considering how much work effects our lives, there are few studies that have had the resources to look at this in depth and in a long-term series analysis like the Whitehall studies. This means we end up with a variety of pieces of a jigsaw but no overall picture. Even the pieces are contradictory, which leads into impossible sense-making of what is truly going on. The Swedes have been interested in workplace bullying for a long time, being the leaders in research and scholarly work (for instance, Einarsen, 1999). They have found that there is also long-term depression that outlasts a bullying episode. The Whitehall studies do show psychiatric morbidity, again associated with lower grades; it is a pity that they did not take into account bullying behaviours that would have existed at that time. You have to look deeply into managerial behaviour to understand what is truly going on in their minds.

When we venture out into our first job, we have no idea what is going to happen. We are not prepared to enter such a vicious world as a young adult. Ideas such as internships and work experience are preparatory in some way, but we do not tell our children what really goes on, neither do we arm them with effective measures to prevent workplace violence.

We have learnt that giving children sex education has reduced to some extent the number of teenage pregnancies, but we fail to teach them about what to expect in the workplace. Such a syllabus could contain strategies to cope with life in the lowest work echelon; how to deal with a bully; how to identify depression and anxiety; how to perform under stress; and how to whistle-blow safely. When I share my theory with others who are in the educational environment, they often say we should be teaching this in our schools! Of course we should. And I would be happy to have input into such a project. If it means we can redesign our workplaces so that these bad behaviours are curtailed then we can win the fight against workplace violence perpetrated against the unwary and the ill-equipped, which is all of us in our very first job.

This book describes behaviour that is opposite to what is found in the average workplace. It is a guide to what good management is and what it is fundamentally about. This is a handbook designed for those who wish to become managers, those who are already managers but having difficulties, those who design MBA and other business programs, human resources people, and just the likes of you and me who are interested in the dynamics of workplaces. In other words, those who are concerned with propagating good management. It is sadly a rarity.

We have seen a burst of activity by scholars trying to understand management from the 1970s onwards. Many fields of research, in psychology, sociology, social psychology, economics and even politics, have all had their say on business management. But still, after all these years of intensive effort we cannot put our finger on the concept. We know what they are meant to do, it is written in their job descriptions, but a good manager? That is where the effort ends up confused. It is not possible to write it down in a job description: applicants would laugh at the wording 'be a good manager'. How can that be done? Let alone measure job performance? Well, the good news is we can write down what it means: it solely ties up with the concept of respect. This popped up in the middle of my research and I explored it further and discovered a simple but elegant formula for any manager to become a really good manager.

The function of management

A manager is often described as a steward of an organisation and fundamentally will look after an organisation and its resources; this includes those who work within the organisation. The role of managers came into being with the beginnings of the agrarian revolution approximately 8,000 years ago. There came a need for someone to look after extra unused food resources after the traditional hunting and gathering of food came to an end. The previous co-operatively based social system gave way to producing more food than the extended family could eat within a few days. As soon as there was surplus production over and above what was to be consumed, certain people were appointed by the group leader to look after the resources on behalf of the community. For instance, a shepherd looking after the community's flock of sheep. Later there came elders and leader-kings who claimed all the resources in a short period of time. Many Mesopotamian pottery pieces and stones were covered with writing. These are in fact lists of resources, the start of basic accounting, which the manager had to provide, or in the more up-to-date phrase, 'account for'.

We can trace the development of the managerial function of stewardship of assets together with accounting, in the changes from the Neolithic era. And these twin functions have expanded into today's world with the addition of six more core functions. According to Quinn (Quinn, 1988) there are eight managerial functions of a good steward of an organisation. These include monitoring and tending to the administrative detail; co-ordinating activity; brokering resources through networking within and outside the organisation; ensuring production of work; directing others; enhancing innovation; understanding and mentoring of the human element in the workplace; and facilitating commitment with diverse people or units of work.

It does not take much imagination to see that some of these early managers would have taken advantage of their position and been fraudulent, and indeed the earliest record of a case was recorded in about 360 BC (Calhoun, 1924). It involved Xenothemis, a sea captain who became involved with an insurance scam. He was in collusion with a merchant who wanted to stage the sinking of Xenothemis' ship and claim for the 'lost' cargo. Even in those early days, schemes were in place to defraud the people of Athens by not actually sending the cargo and then claiming the insurance which was set up by the traders in the first place. The goods in reality were stored at the departure point, so there would be no actual loss. The passengers overheard crew members talking about the scuttling of their ship in the middle of the Mediterranean, and they mutinied and took over the ship. The merchant involved was killed and the captain survived only to land himself in prison, as it was deemed that being told what to do was not an excuse.

Most managers pretend

In our social history there are archetypes of good and evil, the stuff that fairy tales are made of and fables to disseminate moral stories. Jung identified the Trickster as being one of the dominant archetypes that appear in our literature and thinking. There is a need for our psyches, he proposed, to develop an archetype so that we can identify a part of ourselves that we do not wish to acknowledge. It is as if there is a propensity in all of us to steal and deceive others. The archetype's purpose is to put it in our minds that we may admire the trickery involved, say with a magician, but fundamentally we believe that it is dishonest. Therefore, the concept of managerial fraud is able to be defined and discussed; at least that is what I thought when I started my study.

What I was amazed at was the lack of anything substantial, including there being no definition of managerial fraud. The literature confined itself to employee or occupational fraud, not differentiating that managers commit this deception as well. Even with the Association of Certified Fraud Examiners' annual reports (ACFE, 2018) on the state of business affairs in the USA, managerial fraud has not been teased out of the figures presented. That meant I had to put together a definition of managerial fraud myself, as if this was a new phenomenon! The Trickster actually evaded us from our conceptual development in the workplace. This is suggested by the very light sentences that fraudulent managers received before the collapse of Enron in the United States. It was called 'white collar' fraud, and this was seen as not as bad as other types of stealing. The ACFE reports did not even use that term, as 'white collar' is a sociological term that denotes managers and clerks, that is, in a typical manufacturing setting, those individuals who are not part of the means of production but who regulate it.

The Balinese, a people that I have intensively researched, have the notion of the Trickster in their religious ceremonies. They understand the world in terms of good and evil and that we contain both parts; therefore, if someone does something bad, the bad side is showing. One of their most important ceremonies is that of Nyepi – the day of silence, the day before teenage boys and young adult males gather together to fight the Ogoh-Ogoh, which represents the bad spirits located in the depths of the earth. The large, horrifying statues are carried to their death, which is a burning usually on the beach, or if inland by a river or a spring. These are terrifying effigies, and they take months of hard work to make. Once the Ogoh-Ogohs have been burnt, the earth is cleansed and that means that the good spirits can come down and walk upon it without fear. Everyone stays indoors on Nyepi, and there is no talking or eating or travelling. Even the airport of Denpasar is closed. Each family has just one candle to light their night time. The silence is time to reflect on their deeds over the last year. The children are let off these restrictions, but all others are under strict observation by the local religious police. The children, while being saved from the rigours of Nyepi, learn very early on that we all have the bad spirits as well as good spirits at hand. Furthermore, the bad spirits must not be indulged and must be kept away. The strength of Nyepi is that on the following day there is an asking of forgiveness from any person who has been wronged in the past year. This is usually after the morning ceremony and the trip is undertaken with foods which are offered to the gods. The thing that makes this stand out is that the person who has been wronged is obligated to accept the gifts and forgive the person concerned.

This creates a balance of right and wrong, through forgiveness and reparation. Therefore, the Trickster is kept at bay for another year. I asked once when we were undertaking a blessing of our office why were they throwing away the small offerings to the bad spirits. I had noted that there was a deliberate move to carry these tiny offerings away. They included a small bowl of their home brewed alcoholic drink of *tuak*, and the reply was that the bad spirits will be tricked into taking those offerings about 20 meters away from the building, and therefore not visit us. The Trickster is therefore tricked through the artful ways of the Balinese. I will refer to forgiveness and reparation further in this book, as it is an important part of a Respectful Manager's morality.

But first I must set out and explain the theory that cracks the code of silence and deception among managers. This will make clearer how the Trickster managers work in our organisations. They may not be stealing the business's money, but they are up to no good. And the sad thing is that many do not realise that they are doing this and for the ones that do, the immense amount of harm that they commit.

2   How the Respectful Manager type emerged

This chapter introduces the brand new Executive Impression Management theory. I will try to explain it without the technical jargon that is always a feature of social science research. Ideally, even a layperson will be able to understand, as the theory is both elegant and simple, looking at underlying factors that have been touched on but mostly ignored by scholars and commentators.

Good practice

For many decades now, there have been ideas developed to help us understand good practice management (for example, Sutton, 2010). The problems with these theories are that a clever manager can read the textbook, learn what is required but in reality, continue to be the type of manager that no one wants. If a manager is aspiring to the top ranks it may suit him to adopt the latest strategy so as to appear to be a 'good' manager. Many co-workers will complain that the manager knows the words but does not 'walk the talk'. They may see through the deception but often their bosses will not. Therefore, promotion takes place for these managers while discontentment and despair permeates the workplace.

Lack of predictive power

Another problem with these theories is that they do not seem to be able to predict in short or long term, what type of management behaviour will arrive with a new manager. Lack of predictive power is a disturbing fact, as the adoption of certain behaviours will confuse others at times of promotion, or even at the selection process of recruitment, as to who the manager really is. For instance, a manager may use the right words at interview in order to gain entry to an organisation, and this can lead to severe disruption within businesses and non-profits whereby the manager having access to the firm's assets will steal, even for years on end. At best, the new recruit works inefficiently and will waste the organisation's assets.

Bias

We have also seen theories that emphasise masculine Anglo-Saxon behaviours, perhaps subconsciously, and thereby exclude women and those of a different ethnic background. Some very early management theory, for instance Frederick Taylor's work *The Principles of Scientific Management* (1911), started out with the premise of managers being male. The scientists themselves were male and wore white coats to differentiate themselves from male managers. In the 1950s John Maynard Keynes warned us of the problem of gendered management in a different context: 'The ideas of economists and political philosophers, both when they are right and when they are wrong, are more powerful than is commonly understood', he wrote,

> Indeed the world is run by little else. Practical men, who believe themselves to be quite exempt from any intellectual influences are usually the slaves of some defunct economist …. It is ideas not vested interests, which are dangerous for good or evil.
>
> Keynes (1953: 306, reprinted 2007)

The bias here is demonstrated by the use of the phrase 'Practical men', and the language is layered with rational logic which appeals to those with an internal decision making process of logic. It does not however, appeal to women who tend to have a decision making process based on values (see the Myers Briggs Type Indicator or MBTI, described in Myers and Myers, 1995). Without going into too much detail, it has been subsequently found that there is a gendered basis for the different types of decision making with males using logic, thus expressing 'thinking'; whereas women make decisions on values, which are expressed as 'feeling' when making important decisions. For those who use this type of discourse they are, maybe unintentionally, excluding women from management, as it has always been taken to be a rational science. The theory of the MBTI demonstrates that the same-resulting decision can be made by either using the 'thinking' or the 'feeling' function; the distinction is simply of using a different pathway to end up with the same conclusion. The 'feeling' function has nothing to do with being emotional, which is another usage of discourse to exclude women from higher management.

In addition, society becomes dismissive of those who fall unexpectedly on the opposite function, for example, with men using their 'feeling' function often labelled as 'softies' and women using their 'thinking' function as 'bitches'. The point is that neither gender determines the type of decision making; it is a clustering effect that the MBTI Institute has observed about gender. More recent management theories allow for the fact that some people will make decisions based on values, as this permits care of the environment and the community to be as important to organisations as just making money. This is particularly true in the trend towards corporate social responsibility and recognising the polluting effect on the environment of irresponsible manufacturing. Even some shareholders require ethics in their investments, so that no money is invested in companies that break community values, such as the use of child labour.

Sense-making

Another precondition of a good social theory is that it make common sense. It has to do so to those looking at the problems of management. This is bit of a trap for those trying to understand management behaviour, as it makes the rational selection of a theory biased due to the nearness of the concepts that the reader is used to. The latest jargon can be a trap due to the trendiness of the words within the field of management. If we talk about time and motion studies, we automatically think of men in white coats. Men in white coats tend to be symbolic of medicine, and this leads to the perception of a health model of sick versus healthy organisations. Recently there has been a plethora of studies on toxic organisations, but in fact the underlying theory is lacking in substance, because how can an organisation be determined as sick or healthy? A shareholder will only judge on share value, like a thermometer, whereas the truth may very well be that the organisation is far ahead of its time with its products (for example, Apple).

Organisations can be bureaucratic, or anarchic, or be places of conflict between managers, but are they all toxic? Internal behaviour factors, such as rate of employee turnover, are suggestive of toxicity, but not necessarily indicative. I have known companies that have high rates of turnover due to massive change within a redesigned organisation. These may result in one-off wave of resignations or redundancies, but these are not due to toxicity.

Being able to refer to a common sense-making allows the theory to be utilised easily within the social context of management. If a theory can be absorbed easily by the person presented with it, there is more chance that it will be accepted. Complex theories tend to lead individuals ending up in ideological debates rather than seeing the usefulness of their content.

Robust and valid

In addition, theories have to be robust and valid. The strength of the concepts are checked within the qualitative methodology, as well as validity, such as in this study. If the theory is less than robust, for instance if it does not apply to all situations, then it is not a theory, merely a group of hypotheses or ideas thrown up by the research. Triangulation of themes is an important part of the qualitative researcher's job, and if not done properly it can lead to the theory being discredited in the outside world. Quantitative methodologies are more used to validity testing with statistical tools, but these can only be used to test a theory rather than explore the theory itself. This leads to questions of randomness of samples used. In social psychology as well as business theory, it is students who are the focus of much testing. What the validity should really be restricted to, is how well these students score. There cannot be an application to what actual business managers may think or do.

So, with all of these factors in mind, we turn to the new and exciting theory of Executive Impression Management. It certainly has predictive power, is useful and makes sense, and is robust and valid. Coupled with the fact that the theory came about accidentally, it adds value to the proposition that Executive Impression Management may actually be the real motivation behind management. Let me tell you how this came about.

I was looking at the research question of who could I trust as a manager. This was due to a pressing concern that I had within my own business of providing locum managers to small businesses. I was besieged by over 200 people all wanting to be locum managers; almost all looked worthy and all desperately wanted the temporary employment. I have a fairly good intuition, and have recruited many people in my career, but the stakes were much higher here. For a bad locum manager to be placed by me could wreck the small business, but one failure would mean death to my own business. This made the question all the more urgent and I needed answers that I could trust. What I did was use my Ph.D. studies to supply those answers.

Multi-disciplinary approach

Not only was this a fortuitous opportunity to explore the literature recording what others had found before me, but I happened to have a broad social science background due to my previous studies. My undergraduate education was in a brand-new degree, Social Administration, which is like a management degree but for public organisations and non-profits. We were the guinea pigs who had to attain very high standards, so the course co-ordinator loaded up our curriculum. At the time, we students groaned with the work load, but now I am extremely grateful as I have become acquainted with a wide range of literature and scholarly work. The same thing took place in my master's degree course, even though this time I was part of the second cohort to graduate. The other factor that made my education outstanding is that in both settings we were in small groups, which encouraged us to ask questions rather than fall asleep in lectures. Therefore, in my research I was able to jump into the various literatures undaunted, in order to help me understand what was going on.

I looked at social psychology, economics, politics, criminology, deviancy and sociology, but no one could give me the answer as to whom I could trust. What I did then was to look at the worst-case scenario of bad management – long term, huge frauds by managers. How on earth could thefts by managers be hidden from their firms for so long? Here I turned to Impression Management theory (Goffman, 1959) which talked about how people use social artifices to present themselves to others. I felt that something must have gone wrong in the case of managerial fraud – why didn't the co-workers suspect something? Thus, my venture into discovering Executive Impression Management theory began.

Unique study

To add to the exploration of this unique type of deception I did two things which had not been done before. First, I chose to interview the co-workers of managerial fraudsters rather than the fraudsters themselves; the other twist was to compare their experiences with those of another group of co-workers who worked alongside non-fraudster managers. I found two factors of power and consistency which produced five types of managerial Executive Impression Management. I will discuss this later at some length as it is an important part of what makes a Respectful Manager.

Expert deceivers

The answer was that fraudsters are experts at deceiving others; once you are in their spotlight of influence, you cannot see through what is happening to you. Their impression management tactics are so strong that a boss of such a manager will fight to the bitter end of disbelief until faced with the bald facts that their manager truly is a fraudster. This shocking realisation then starts a process of breaking down trust within nearly everyone who is connected to the manager, who stopped trusting others as a consequence. Meanwhile, the fraudster manager continues to defraud other organisations even while out on bail, spinning a tale of woe to other business owners. Why would anyone employ an alleged, arrested and charged fraudster? This action demonstrates the power that these managers have over their organisations.

This is not about the gullibility of those working alongside the fraudster manager. Gullibility implies that there is a lack of discernment. It is seen as a weakness and a serious character flaw, so that such people can be taken advantage of by others. However, gullibility is not the case. It has to be understood that Executive Impression Management is so strong that it is almost impossible to see through it. Why is this so? The reason lies in our innate desire to trust. A baby must trust his mother for food, security and safety. We grow up into being trusting adults. However, this can be disrupted when a significant other interferes with this natural instinct. For instance, there may be a family member who abuses that trust, at school a teacher may go against the rules of trust, or school friends, by bullying. The problem is that even those with disrupted patterns of trust can still be taken in by the fraudster managers. Furthermore, I always counsel those who have been deceived by such managers to have therapeutic intervention as trust is so fundamental to our well-being and happiness.

Incredibly, for those working with non-fraudster managers the disruption of trust was to the same level, namely severe. The co-worker is aware that something is wrong, but is not able to correctly identify the cause. Four of the five types are referred to as 'malevolent' in the typology, and if you are working with a malevolent manager there is little happiness or well-being as bullying is rife, as well as other forms of emotional abuse.

With the Respectful Manager, all is well. Working with this type does not produce any disruption of trust. In fact, the opposite occurs with the comfort of trust being reciprocated. Being trusted in a workplace is like sunshine. People feel better and work better. When a piece of work goes wrong, the Respectful Manager treats the individual with respect, so that learning can take place and the mistake can be rectified.

3 Use of power and consistency as factors of the Respectful type

Here I will describe and explore the characteristics of a Respectful Manager. The other, malevolent types are dealt with elsewhere (Sheridan 2014, 2016) at length, but it will be necessary to briefly look at them so as to understand the underlying factors of power and consistency.

Many people ask me how I came up with the typology. In order to understand what was going on, I had mapped out all the variables, or clusters of meaning as we say in qualitative research, on my office wall. This lead to a giant overview of well over 2,000 units of meaning. Of course, there is computer software that does this as well, but I can highly recommend a large wall and sticky tape to any qualitative researcher. Reading the overview led me to the understanding that there were two variables that seemed to control the rest, namely Power and Inconsistency, and this generated a model of how these two factors determine the type of management behaviour.

Power in the workplace

Academics have already come up with a useful list of types of power used in the workplace (French and Raven, 1960) which has been added to since the first list was developed. But few have talked about the usage of power, apart from the conflict theorists who have framed power differently. They see it as an inevitability of capitalism and any decent managers out there are pawns of the owners of production. But here, on the wall, I realised that there were two ways that the managers used their power. It was a subtle difference, but an important one. Let me give you an example to allow you to stay with me on this.

One type of workplace power is coercion. That is a harsh name for what can happen in the workplace. What I found was that some managers used this in a superior manner: 'Do what I say or I will fire you!' But others used coercion in a very different way: 'I like you very much, do this and you won't get fired.' The manager still retains the power to fire someone, but the latter statement is more underhanded. When I looked at the factor from this point of view there was a definite trend of superior use of power and a different more subtle, manipulative underhandedness. As it was the opposite of superior use, I labelled it the inferior use of power.

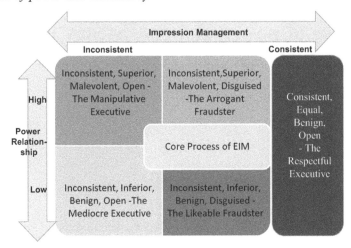

Figure 3.1 The overall core process of Executive Impression Management

This led to the map on the wall lighting up for me. The two variants were there in practically everything that was said by the co-workers. There was a remnant section who talked about their manager in an equal way, including subordinates, and joked how their manager could be told off by them and the manager would take it easily on the chin. This is not showing weakness by the manager or staff that would be acting 'above their station', it is a genuine observation of how power is used by that type of manager. Equality is a wonderful thing, and not often seen in organisations as everyone gets caught up with their hierarchical status. This hierarchy results in sometimes being geographically distant by having a separate head office, or just a door to find the company's executives in their suites rather than the open plan offices of their co-workers.

Putting the remainder of power equality statements aside, I was able to deduce from the data that certain types of managers would use power in the same way, but it was either in a superior or inferior manner. This related to fraudster managers as well as their non-fraudster counterparts. So the typology of Arrogant Fraudsters and Tyrant Managers came into being. Both used their power in a superior manner, the co-workers felt below them in status, because their managers exuded this. The Arrogant Fraudsters and Tyrants seemed to possess psychopathic tendencies, ruling over people, dictating the way things had to be done, openly firing those who disagreed.

Then we had those managers who were seen by their co-workers to be using power underhandedly, that is, in an inferior manner. And again, another two types popped out, the Likeable Fraudsters and the Mediocre Managers who were non-fraudulent. The co-workers saw that they used such devices as flattery, having favourites, manipulation, excluding people from information shared and so on. The Likeable Fraudster was so much liked that when their frauds were exposed, co-workers were devastated, as they realised that they had been merely groomed by the fraudster managers to cover their fraudulent activities, that the relationship that he or she had with them was a sham. Similarly, the co-workers felt emotionally abused by the Mediocre Managers, and felt that they were only pawns in the game to move their manager higher up the organisation.

For the remaining few managers there was equality of power shared by all in the organisation. And these managers never abused the power vested in them by their status. These managers attracted all sorts of statements of loyalty, trustworthiness, authenticity and morality, which I will go into later.

Thus the five types of managers emerged using different types of Executive Impression Management.

Consistency

The other factor was consistency. The co-workers noted whether a manager was consistent or inconsistent in their behaviour. The ones that were totally consistent in the observations of their co-workers came to be the Respectful Manager type. And you can see by Table 3.1 that only the Respectful Manager is consistent. There is no room for being a bit consistent with these observations regarding Respectful Managers. It is like being pregnant, you are or you are not. Similarly, with consistency shown by this group of managers, they were completely consistent.

The Tyrant and Mediocre Manager types however, were openly inconsistent. The co-workers did not know what was coming next as their managers were so inconsistent. This led to them trying to second guess what their manager was going to do or say. At other times routines were upset by a sudden change in direction from their manager. Tyrants were exceptionally so, as they could fire an employee if they happen to question the manager. The common saying of 'It's my way or the highway' is typical of the Tyrant Manager.

The Mediocre Manager, however, is still openly inconsistent but in a much more underhanded way. If you do not support them you can still be evicted from your workspace, but it will be done in a roundabout manner. One of the notorious ways that a Mediocre Manager will resort to is that they will make

Table 3.1 The five types of Executive Impression Management

Executive impression management type	Usage of power	Consistency of behaviour	Attitude of their behaviour to organisations
The Arrogant Fraudster	Superior	Inconsistent	Malevolent
The Likeable Fraudster	Inferior	Inconsistent	Malevolent
The Tyrant Manager	Superior	Inconsistent	Malevolent
The Mediocre Manager	Inferior	Inconsistent	Malevolent
The Respectful Manager	Equality	Consistent	Benign

the position redundant. Suddenly the target is ousted with little or no recourse to reinstatement. Another way that the Mediocre Manager shows inconsistency is through having favourites. A manager should treat their co-workers all the same way, not have the chosen few or one.

Now what made it interesting is that when co-workers said that only occasionally was the manager inconsistent it was the fraudster of either type who used that sort of behaviour. All the ducks were in a row, except one, and that was noticed. The inconsistency was brought up by saying that it was odd, merely a minor curiosity. It may have been something like noticing that the manager lied when he or she was caught out on something trivial. Lying, even white lies, was seen as being odd, as well as buying expensive office furniture, losing their temper and shouting at their staff – all were among many examples of inconsistency where the prevailing attitude was that the manager was a nice person. As I have alluded to earlier, consistency is a dichotomous variable, it is either there or it is not. Therefore, when the co-workers found out these little oddities it was most confusing for them. The answer is that the manager was wearing a strong mask of deception, but it cracked over time; I found that it was impossible to wear the mask without some cracks showing through to the real person underneath.

Impression management

A word here for the theoreticians who know the theory of Impression Management, which my exploratory study was predicated on. Goffman (1959) identified the social artifice that all of us use in our interaction with others. The only time that we do not use impression management is when we are alone. It is a natural part of our humanness that we use this social artefact, so that when we are presented to the president of the United States or the British monarch, a person will probably be on their 'best behaviour' and act a little bit different from normal day to day. But both behaviours, best or normal, are still part of our impression management, and they do not differ due to the element of authenticity. It is very similar to how we dress up to go out to dinner: jeans and a T-shirt is inappropriate, so we put on our best clothes. We are still the same people underneath. Assuming no multiple personality disorders, we operate within the boundaries of who we are. It is authenticity that keeps us solid. So, if a person does not tell lies for instance, then we would expect no lies to be told to the president of the United States or the queen of England by that individual.

Lying

Obviously, many people tell lies, in fact an awful lot of people tell an awful amount of lies and it is commonplace. But if telling lies is normal behaviour, then it will be incorporated into their impression management. Thus, the Tyrant and the Mediocre Managers tell lies, whether overtly or underhandedly, they always do this, it would be a shock to see otherwise. In fact, it would go against the typology and that manager would have to be investigated further to ensure that there is not a false negative result. However, as the theory of Executive Impression Management is predicated upon interaction in the workplace, it is only the Respectful Managers who do not lie, ever.

In the study, when co-workers were talking about their manager who turned out to be a fraudster, it was a shock to them to see this aberrant behaviour. And in every case, it was ignored. No one thought to check it out further. What the fraudster manager is doing is frantically trying to keep looking the same, but they cannot keep up the deception for long periods of time. Reviewing what the co-workers said, these little cracks in the mask started to appear within months of arrival into the new position. Small incongruities must raise the alarm that it is likely that the manager concerned is fraudulent.

As I have come to realise, as have organisations that I deal with, if you have a manager who is in charge of finance in some manner, for instance, accounts, procurement, contracts, and he or she lies, then isolate that person immediately from that function and hold a spot audit. Do not have a liar in charge of money as you will live to regret it. And as iterated, Respectful Managers do not lie, and they are the ones that should be holding the purse strings, not any of the other types.

The reason why the four types of malevolent managers lie is that they think that they can get away with it through their power in the organisation. It is a bold move for a person to take them on about the lie; it is very much like the fairy tale of the Emperor's New Clothes, when it took a little boy who had no association with the palace system to shout out that the Emperor was not wearing any clothes. One of the best whistleblowers in recent history was an accountant, Sherron Watkins, at Enron in the 2000s (Watkins, 2003) who went to the chairman of the board and proved that there was fraudulent activity going on. Unfortunately, she did not know that the chairman was in on the deception as well and he was about to eject her from the organisation when the whole edifice came tumbling down and the main players either died or ended up in prison within a few years. The truth ultimately came out; it exemplifies that trying to change the reality of one person's truth with a lie is not a particularly good way to live a corporate life, as any particular lie has to be shored up with others and so on. One lie leads to others, maybe thousands in a managerial career.

A word about lying, as it is so commonplace. There is no such thing as a good lie. We soothe ourselves by saying that it is told to keep the peace, or that the person concerned would be devastated to hear otherwise. Sometimes the truth will hurt, but it is how it is said that can make the truth more presentable than bald facts. To use the perennial example of a wife asking her husband when trying on new clothes: 'Does my bottom look big in this?' The husband feels he is in a no-win situation: owning up to the fact with 'Yes' means the conversation will lead to a big argument. To say 'No' means that the wife chooses clothes that do in fact emphasise her pear-shaped figure. But what is the best thing to do? To stick with the truth. The husband has options of saying 'I prefer the other clothes' or 'Try this other dress on.' He does not have to say a bald 'Yes'. Sometimes keeping silent is the best option, or even changing the subject. At other times, as often happens in management, the bad news has to be delivered. Answers to the question 'Will I get promotion after submitting this report?' have to be true. And if it is a negative reply, say so but add the pathway into making the promotion. People can accept criticism if it is given in a helpful way.

There are some people for whom rejection is devastating. Therefore, their manager has to be extremely careful how the news is delivered. A good manager would have picked this up about an individual. In my case, due to my background, someone asking me if I wanted a piece of toast would read as a rejecting statement to me! This sounds like a busy manager would have to be a mind reader. Fortunately, that is not so. Anyone who is concerned with a co-worker should be interested to see how this person works and to assist whenever they can. If bad news has to be given, then as Respectful Managers always try to develop their subordinates, they will offer a pathway through that rejection. They want their people to grow and be successful, and they want to be part of that, doing their job in the best way possible.

Honesty and integrity

Therefore, Respectful Managers are honest in their dealings with their co-workers. It is the way that they are built; their authenticity precludes lies being told and their compassion assists people through their difficulties in the workplace. Of course, we know that there are emotionally needy people out there, and the manager cannot become their therapist, but again, defining the boundary of helpfulness, therapeutic intervention has to be left to trained individuals. This is one of the reasons that if an organisation has an employee assistance plan, the co-worker can be thoughtfully referred to a counsellor to assist their personal development. Just as health care is important to a caring organisation, and in some countries this is the only way health care can be delivered through the company joining a health insurance plan, psychiatric care must be provided as well. Depression is one disease that has come about through centuries of ignorance and abuse. Recognising that the individual may need help is all part of the manager's job. To be able to say to a co-worker: 'Look, I have heard that you have been through a rough time, how about we talk about this later in my office after work?' gives the individual room to explore their feelings and feel safe with that manager.

One of the best ways I have used when faced with a difficult question is to clarify further with an 'In what way?' request. Usually the person is able to fill in with the details and give enough information so that I can formulate a better, more helpful answer. Most people are trained to give a Yes or No response, yet life is not like that. It is far subtler. And once you understand the basis of the question and why it is so important to the person, then a more caring response can be given.

Let me explain further. I think that we can all agree that examination marks can give the student the wrong impression, and that a 51 per cent pass on a difficult exam is in fact a brilliant mark, whereas on an easier test 91 per cent can be seen as a failure. Young people brand themselves as a success or failure based on these marks, yet they may mean nothing as the marks do not represent the context of the test. It is the context that is so important. Similarly, gaining a new customer for a sales person may be absolute joy, but in fact new customers who turn out to be demanding and turn processes upside down are not a joy, and soon have to be dealt with by drawing boundaries. In my own businesses, I learnt very quickly that a new customer had to be an educated customer so that we could cater properly to their needs. I learnt to say no even to large corporations whereas other small businesses would have grabbed them. But I knew that joy would turn into an overwhelming factor that could lead the business into bankruptcy if their single client did not pay on time. Let others go bankrupt; keep with good respectful customers who pay on time and always want your product. So all in all, honesty is really the best policy in business management.

4 Description and characteristics of the Respectful Manager

When I asked co-workers about their managers, the ones who worked with those who were typed as Respectful completely ran out of words to describe them. I would get one-word replies, such as 'Good!' or 'Great!' After receiving long replies from the other co-workers who worked with malevolent managers, which could fill many pages on just one aspect, I was stunned. No matter what I did, I couldn't get much better than that, and I am a very experienced interviewer! What I learnt from that is that people think that they know when they have a good manager. This was due to the impression management being authentic and that the manager did everything that was expected of him or her, and the audience took the signs in that the manager was 'giving off' that the impression management was correct. But things can go awry in a social interaction, which is why I turned to impression management theory to understand the process better.

Actors and audiences

There are two components to impression management, the actor (the manager) and the audience (co-workers). We use impression management as an audience to vet the manager concerned. It is a two-way process. The manager has to establish the role of manager and fit into the shoes that are pre-designed for a manager to fill. Then the audience has to check the validity of the fit with the assigned role. They do this by looking for little differences in the role and the behaviour of the manager. This is the vital part of impression management, but it is very subtle. People are unaware that this happens, but you can see the two-way process happen immediately when something goes wrong in the role. I have proved this countless times in my talks about Executive Impression Management. I deliberately pop in a slide that is completely incongruous with what I am talking about. The audience must use their role of tact to cover up the gaffe, or more likely, not believe that I am doing a good job in my presentation. Occasionally I get a person who puts up their hand to point out the error, but the audience usually remains stock still, waiting for my next move. When I apologise and then give my explanation that I was showing impression management in operation, there is almost a sigh of relief, that I am not an idiot after all.

This example shows how deep impression management is within our psyches, if we have disbelief the mechanism fails. The actor is exposed, and more importantly, has lost the trust of the audience completely. Now there is no possible bridge to reconcile the actor and the audience. Goffman used many examples to explain the power of impression management and it is enlightening to read how extensive it is in all of our social interaction with others.

Workplace distortion

Now what I found in the workplace is that the natural impression management process is warped through power. This is why I have named this distortion Executive Impression Management; it happens in the workplace and it may happen elsewhere in our human relationships, for example in families, if there is a similar imbalance of power. Goffman's theory relies on power between the actor and the audience being equal, and I was the one that found out that in practice, the two participating parties in the workplace are not equal. This was so much so, that it changed the balance of impression management that Goffman proposed.

Looking at other areas with the co-workers of Respectful Managers I found that there was a well-developed sense of self-awareness with their managers, truthfulness, trust, authenticity and a moral self underneath the behaviours that they witnessed. These qualities are not found with malevolent managers, so it is worthwhile to talk about these attributes as these demonstrate the expectations of the co-workers with the actor.

Acting in truth

Goffman figured that people must 'act in truth' to be participating in impression management. Respectful Managers are trusted that there is no other side to them. Of course, the Malevolent Managers were not so, especially after the fact when lies that are told are found out to be false. Respectful Managers are 100 per cent trusted to always act in truth. There are no lies. As I said earlier, some people will lie all the time. Lies are manipulative, enforcing a different reality upon the listener. Once the lie is found out all trust disappears between the two parties. Therefore, a Respectful Manager will never deceive others. If they do, and you are convinced that this is an exception, then I am sorry but you are mistaken, you have a malevolent manager on your hands and the lie proves it.

Self-awareness

First of all, we will deal with self-awareness. The respondents mentioned that their manager had a fault or two. These faults were not major but could drive a co-worker mad in some instances. One example was that the Respectful Manager was more than aware that his filing skills were terrible. He simply did not return client files into the central system. What happened was that he would make a joke of it together with the co-workers, so that if a file went missing, a quick check was made of the manager's desk and staff would find it there. He tried hard to put files back into the system, but being side tracked, it led to the files being buried under more paperwork. The joking about this fault was self-awareness. The co-workers knew it, and so did he, and he tried to fix it. His hours were long and hard so attending to this detail was onerous, but he still found time to try and do the right thing.

The other part of this self-awareness is that the co-workers feel free to take up this problem with their manager. This is where equality plays into the relationship. If you work with a malevolent manager you will be soon stopped from giving any feedback, as the manager concerned will not allow criticism of any sort. She will see it as interference to the normal routine of using power over or under with her co-workers. The spin-off effect is that the lack of equality felt with a malevolent manager prevents important and sometimes strategically vital information being passed up the hierarchy.

The problem of self-awareness is that we do not want to admit, especially to others, that we are less than perfect. It comes from a deep perception of perfection within ourselves, and if we are flawed then the tighter this perception is maintained within. If a flaw is exposed, we feel ashamed and angry with ourselves and others for allowing this to happen. The truth is that we are not perfect beings, living in this world with all of its influences affects our gentle souls as we grow up and become adults. To achieve 100 per cent perfection is unattainable. Perfection is impossible to achieve living in our world. From small babies we learn that the world is not the perfect Garden of Eden. That some people dislike us for no reason at all, and we take on that shame as marks of flaws in our character.

Maturing as an adult is to realise and understand that we do have faults. While we do not like this process, we can come to terms with it and endeavour to change that part within us that creates this fault. Many people grow up in families who have a warped sense of trust, or have little regard for the law, or their poverty creates a drive for more and more things to have and own. Very few of us have perfect families to grow up in, and if that does happen, what about our education and work? None of those environments will be a clean slate of perfection. Self-awareness is based on accepting the blemishes that we have. That is why counselling and therapeutic interventions often bring a person to realise that the imperfections that they think they have, are actually common and erasable. Once the individual forgives themselves for a particular fault, then they become more mature as they understand that they are fallible. This fallibility means that we understand our nature and accept it and try not to inflict it upon others.

Let's go through a workplace example. Say, a person who feels compelled to correct those around them on their use of English. The English language is an amalgam of many languages and is a hotchpotch of tenses, irregular verbs, spellings that bewitches any non-native or even native speaker into mistakes. If this person has to stop conversations with incorrect grammar, or sends back reports with red lines through the submission, very soon resentment will build up with co-workers. The person concerned will be oblivious to what is going on, as all he or she thinks is that we have to speak and write English perfectly or not at all. Overnight the person is criticised as being pedantic, impossible to work with and highly unpopular in the lunch room chat. Consider one brave soul who approaches the pedant and informs him of what is going on with his peers. There now opens up an opportunity to become aware of the constant criticism. The individual is then able to deny or accept that this is true, and as it is quite anti-social behaviour, the critiques have to be reduced. If the person accepts this awareness of his fault, then he can change or modify that behaviour. If he denies it, then the individual has lost his chance to change, and people will continue to withdraw.

In the Executive Impression Management typology, all the malevolent managers will not accept the hint that the correction of English grammar is antisocial and will continue to use it. Their poor workers then would have to choose to stay or leave depending on how bad that they feel about the ongoing criticism.

The Respectful Managers, though, will take it on board, once it is established that they do this. A quick survey of a few trusted people in the workplace will suffice to establish this as fact, and then the correction can be made. Everyone breathes a sign of relief and the co-workers are lifted as they can see that their manager is improving himself and now can offer suggestions to ease the problem. What happens is that the people around that manager actually help heal the fault and are supportive. If the manager finds that the co-workers are making fun of him, then the manager has to undertake a serious evaluation of why this is happening and make a choice of staying or leaving.

In the above example, there is one type of malevolent manager that must be looked out for, as they can hide their annoyance and use it against the brave person who stepped up. This type of behaviour is noted in the Mediocre type. They will ostensibly follow the correction that has been pointed out, but the person who was brave enough to say this will have a reaction created by the manager or indirectly through his in-crowd of favourites and may find themselves out of a job in a few months' time. They wear their own mask of perfection, as they seemingly accept the critique with good humour but in fact do not like it at all and take their anger underground. For any co-worker, this is dangerous, as ultimately you do not know where you stand with such a manager, eroding all trust in their relationship.

Trust

Trust is the foundation of the impression management process. The actor trusts the audience to react appropriately if the impression management is received properly. The audience in their turn trusts that the actor is not deceiving them. You can imagine the shock that was felt by a few co-workers in my study who were used to working with Respectful Managers and then found themselves in a situation where their new manager was malevolent and untrustworthy. It led to deep emotional conflict, and one co-worker reported a nervous breakdown. And when these co-workers return to the workforce their trust in any manager is gone, no matter what type the new managers are.

I am always surprised when organisations do little to engender trust in their daily work. There have been attempts through such processes as quality assurance, which produces a written template of what to do, when and how. When I see this working it is very encouraging, as the management is making an attempt to assist their workers in every way. I am not talking about cute ethics statements or corporate values that are often pinned up on the wall in reception. It has to permeate every position in the workplace. In fact, there is no need to put up such notices as everyone knows this, the staff, the customers and suppliers. A quality assured organisation that is truly one, means that you can trust others to do their jobs correctly within reasonable time spans. If there is no trust it means that the organisation is a mess; it may not look it, but I can assure you that it is exactly like a swan appearing to swim gracefully on a pond, whereas beneath the surface it is paddling like crazy to keep up to deadlines for production and meet its customers' expectations. The trust component means that staff are given expected outcomes on a timeline, so that they know what to do and when. Once a manager moves the goalposts the staff lose faith in what is going on and start a withdrawal process mentally if not physically.

Morality

The area of morality is critical for impression management to take place. This implies that both parties are moral and is required for judging the actor's performance. All moral behaviour is tacitly learnt and agreed through taking part in society and social roles. When a doctor hangs up a certificate granting him a licence to practise medicine and it turns out that the certificate is false, patients are, quite rightly up in arms at this deceit.

Morality covers all spheres of human behaviour. This includes sexual behaviour, particularly promiscuity although not necessarily sexual diversity, which is becoming increasingly tolerated these days. It covers what you do to someone has to be what you would want done unto you, so no lies, no cheating, no coveting of things that are the domain of others, no killing and so on. The Ten Commandments are a good base to start, but our social codes are derived from many parts of the world and our diverse history.

Goffman was at pains to point out that it was the group that the actor belonged to which was critical for morality. When a criminal talked to his gang, he would stay in his role of criminal. There could be double takes between the actor and his audience, as if winking at his gang, but this would be perfectly acceptable, as long as all involved knew what was going on. So, morality for these criminals would be that you must look out for yourself, killings or stealing can be done, slanderous and libellous statements could operate.

Conflict arises, though, when an audience works within one moral code and the actor operates in another. This is precisely what happens in the workplace with malevolent managers. These malevolent managers will want to achieve whatever they can for themselves, whereas the hapless audience, which would not only include co-workers but other managers, possibly the board of directors, and shareholders, consider that manager is there to protect and look after the interests and resources of the organisation. This type of disharmony can be recorded and used as evidence, as it is imperative that such dissonance be obliterated. If the tone at the top is that of a bunch of crooks, then it will only be the Respectful Managers who will look out of context.

The other thing about morality is that it is unconscious, so it is difficult to see. That is why it is important to step back and look at the behaviour as an outsider, as difficult as that may be when under the Executive Impression Management spotlight of a Malevolent Manager. I often suggest to people who are wanting to evaluate their manager as objectively as possible, to look at the manager's morals. For example, if the manager is having an affair with a co-worker, usually one or other is married and therefore the affair is against our moral code. For an authentic relationship in the place of work, that is between eligible parties, one or other has to move out of that workplace. It can be sorted out between them which one goes. This has to happen for others to feel equal to that manager; an affair interrupts this process and has to be stopped. Until one of them leaves, it must be made clear to all that the relationship has formed and steps are being put into place to ensure no favouritism is at large. The Respectful Manager will always do his or her utmost to ensure stability in the moral code for the workplace.

For those in affairs with a married partner, then it has to stop. Sorry, but it has to stop out of respect for their co-workers. A Malevolent Manager would sometimes not care what others would say as they do not value equality. The ones likely to try and conceal but still continue are the manipulative managers who use their power 'under' people. This points to a Likeable Fraudster or a Mediocre Manager. As most workplaces have their share of the latter, I would most likely assume that this manager is using Mediocre Executive Impression Management.

Therefore, going against the moral code of the workplace is a warning that all is not well with that manager. A Respectful Manager will always look after their people first. We never know when or who we are likely to fall in love with, and it does happen often in the workplace, but I have had to counsel too many people on this who end up losing their jobs when the affair ends. It is said that some will sleep to the top, and of course it does happen. This kind of ruthless behaviour is frowned upon by many, but not by the person who is set out on doing this. Probably this behaviour is one of the suite of behaviours that form the Tyrant Manager or the Arrogant Fraudster's profile. It is very typical of the corporate psychopath, of either gender, to use their physical attractiveness in this way. Their pathway to the top is littered with many failed marriages and lovers who are too frightened to take them to the authorities. If we look at con men who do this as a daily occupation, the charmed women are always blinded to the fact that their lover is a fraudster, and there is no doubt that the same story would happen in the workplace.

Many procurement frauds are similar in the way that fraudulent managers take in other co-workers to allow their illegal activity to progress. Procurement fraud relies on outside contractors and middle people in accounts or in the warehouse to ignore what is going on. Clearly this is immoral behaviour, and not through any choice, the individual may be pressured to do this by the Malevolent Manager. Again, it points to morality. Does your behaviour, no matter how you have been pressured to do it, go against your moral code? Then report it immediately, ideally on a hotline and anonymously so there is no retribution. If there is no such whistleblowing system in place, alerting the supplier can help, or finding a Respectful Manager in another department or unit will be helpful.

Almost all conundrums in the workplace of the 'What should I do?' variety fall under the heading of morality. Our society allows for breaks in the moral code such as the ends justifies the means. Thinking that stealing one paper clip is not going to bring down a multinational corporation is true, but if all the employees did that every day, huge profits would walk out the door, and your job with it. Saying that 'Everyone does it', does not justify any sort of behaviour that breaks our moral code. It is used often as a defence, but it must not be allowed to interfere with an investigation of a particular practice. If it is true everyone does it, then you have received a large amount of corporate intelligence to change the situation. Only bad managers would allow and condone this type of mass behaviour. Be careful though, perks of the job may well be legitimate. Two centuries ago, it was a common practice that agricultural labourers could go to harvested fields and pick up any wheat that they found. This is a tradition and it has been upheld for a long time. But here is the thing, the landowner agreed with this practice as it meant no loss to them, and they allowed this practice to happen. Paperclips are different, as any person responsible for stationery will tell you, and while the organisation may turn a blind eye, or write off the loss as a tax break, it is still wrongdoing. Table 4.1 shows the characteristics of impression management to work successfully comparing Malevolent and Respectful managers.

Training and development

A characteristic of Respectful Managers is that they will always look after their people, as much as they can. This includes training and development. One Respectful Manager trained a receptionist into a bookkeeper, as he noted her intelligence was far beyond that required for reception work. But if that person was better off being a receptionist then the training development may very well be inclined to developing good communication skills, organisation skills, which probably will be at a high standard to begin with, but there is always room for improvement. I have known receptionists to be sent on

Table 4.1 Checklist of Executive Impression Management behaviours by managers

Criterion for 'normal' impression management	Malevolent EIM	Respectful EIM
Acting in truth	Not present, will lie	Present, never lies
Authenticity	May seem authentic but there are breaks	Continual, no breaks
Morality	Immoral	Moral
Self-awareness	Unaware	Aware
Trust	Untrustworthy and does not trust others	Trustworthy and is trusting of others

conflict management courses, in case an incoming caller is obnoxious and so on. For organisations doing this there is often an unintended side effect in that they retain their people.

We all know how much it costs to refill a position, the advertising, the interviewing and subsequent induction into the workplace. Yet Malevolent Managers do not care about the cost and fire others indiscriminately, or in many cases determinedly discriminatory, getting rid of employees that do not fit their culture of the macho manager. Both men and women managers get sucked into these malevolent ways and can easily copy that sort of behaviour.

Good managers keep their staff and accommodate them if they need to take leave for whatever reason, even retaining them part-time if possible, and willingly keep them beyond retirement age. Respectful Managers keep their staff, and their co-workers understand this and are intensely loyal to their manager. This pays off with lower HR costs and higher profits as happy employees are productive employees. In a recent study researchers were able to document a 12–20 per cent increase in productivity (Oswald et al., 2015) which details the uplift that many of us experienced managers know. If employees are treated like slaves, then more time is spent by them not working at their capacity, complaining, or even finding other jobs in work time. Absenteeism is high and low output is guaranteed. Treating people poorly often results in workaholism for the few who acquire huge workloads.

Natural stewards

The final characteristic of a Respectful Manager is that they are natural stewards. This is the type that is desperately sought after by shareholders and investors; they need their investment to be looked after and carefully nurtured. Venture capital funds providers look for this characteristic as they want their funds to be returned with dividends. Their due diligence process often has a thorough search regarding management. Unfortunately, many of the managers passing inspection are in fact malevolent but carefully deceive the vetting process. It is my contention that this is the main reason for ventures to fail, all things being equal, as the managers cannot stop their dark sides from taking over. This is referred to as agency theory in management text-books (see George Hendrikse, 2003) and fuels the debate as to whether high bonuses and other monetary incentives should be offered to CEOs. The hope is that the incentive will increase the manager's drive to bring in more profits. The result of this is that many organisations go through several CEOs while assets are stripped, productivity looks better with widespread sackings, and the intellectual property walks away to other more sustainable offerings. I do not think that money is a major drive for a Respectful Manager; they are more interested in impact of their work and helping others through their service or products.

A Respectful Manager would not be participating in this sort of incentive. Just rewards are a mark of respectful management. No bribes are needed to extract performance out of a CEO: a respectful CEO will give their best regardless. Neither do Respectful Managers offer bribes to their people to work at their best. Being fair to all is a necessary component of their basic value of equality. They will not get into bidding wars over staff, neither will they underpay as this demeans the person.

I do, however, hear of many grievances about being underpaid, but that is due to the malevolent management as they are not interested in fairness. Pay scales in some organisations are carefully evaluated and often levels are made available so that everyone knows what others receive. The Respectful Manager is fair and just; it would be extremely unlikely that he or she would be otherwise, unless pressured by the organisation to be so. This can happen in a unit that is away from head office, where there is a little kingdom of respectful management. Wages and salaries are enforced from HQ, but the Respectful Manager will always do his or her best to reward their co-workers accordingly. In this manner, resources are carefully husbanded and not frittered away. Even with the training and development that they give to their staff, they will not be offering this as a sort of gift for good behaviour, which the Malevolent Managers do. Each person is considered for specific training and it is not given as a reward for good behaviour. That will often come in different ways and may not be in monetised incentives. Recognition is often used by a Respectful Manager as they know that rewards can be given in many ways to suit the needs of the person, the awardee. These are the sorts of things that should be taught at management schools but are often lacking.

In times of stress or crisis the Respectful Managers are the best managers. It is their natural caring for people that comes to the fore. I have seen orga-nisations devastated by flood, earthquake, war and other forces. Yet a Respectful Manager will get stuck in, to put things together for their staff as quickly as possible and as humanely as possible. It is not a coincidence that many aid organisations have Respectful Managers at their helm and in the organisation itself. However, there is a proviso to that statement: just because a humanitarian organisation exists it does not mean that the management will be respectful. In fact one of my famous firings happened at a non-profit organisation which I had mistakenly believed was in existence to help others. This was not the case, and I was fired. A hard lesson to learn, but one that helps you to understand that it is the innate respectfulness that marks the organisation, not their mission statement. Malevolent Managers pose as altruistic managers when in fact they are not. You have to do your homework to understand this, which is why I have written this book. Without it, many years of productive work can be wasted.

One last note about Respectful Managers is that organisations must use them for heading risk and audit functions, even at board level. They would have thought about disaster recovery from many different situations, not just the new cyber attacks; their brief would include natural disasters, human disasters such as warfare and economic isolationism, and understand that the greatest risk comes from inside with Malevolent Managers. Most small businesses have a risk plan that runs inside the owner's head, but they do need to think about having a Respectful Manager in a key function so that if anything should happen that manager can step forward. This was the basis of my business in 2002, but the problem for me concerned who could I trust to run a business in the owner's absence. This led to my doctoral research and the discovery of the theory of Executive Impression Management, that now tells us to employ only Respectful Managers and you will be a lot better off than using a Malevolent Manager who will convince you that they are the best one for the role. Ignore what they say, and use the Executive Impression Management code to crack their deceit.

Respectful Managers should be used in all key functions. If there are upcoming Malevolent Managers, the Respectful Managers will be more alert to what could go wrong. Respectful Managers can be wrong themselves, but their judgement overall is very good, and is certainly in the interests of the organisation. My advice is that in any promotion from the ranks the main criteria should be based on those of the Respectful Manager.

There will be Malevolent Managers reading this book to find out what to do and say so they can slip through by looking like a Respectful Manager. Their problem is that no matter how much they try they will show themselves for what they really are through cracks in their presentation of self. Consistency has to be there in the career history, with background checks ensuring there have been no misdemeanours. Sure, there may very well be minor faults in the manager's background. The manager concerned must be asked about this, and then return to the information giver to see if the explanation is correct and or feasible. We do not live in a perfect world, so imperfections must be checked out thoroughly. In fact, background checking managers is basically a blockchain methodology. If there is one malevolent act recorded on the CV, then everything must be reviewed thoroughly to get to the reason why. That's why, if necessary, I go back further into the person's history, even to their childhood, to search for the reason for the malevolent action.

5 The fancy dress ball

How the Malevolent Managers confuse others

This is an important chapter as going to work is very much like going to a fancy dress ball. You may put your workday clothes on, but most managers put on their Executive Impression Management suits ready to manipulate, coerce and force you into doing work that is suboptimal.

It really does not have to be like that at all. Those who work with Respectful Managers enjoy their roles in the organisation and feel trusted and respected. If you have a manager who is less than that, your life will become horrible. This means that you will hate going to work. When there, you will feel forced to do your job, any credit that you deserve will be taken away by a Malevolent Manager, you will not feel trusted as there will be much double checking and even spying. In my research several co-workers felt that they were mistreated by the system at work and some even had complete breakdowns due to the stress and maltreatment that they suffered. This is serious emotional violence with associated poor mental health outcomes.

The problem for most of us is that we become used to the violence in our workplaces. Many may say, what violence? For one thing, it is usually very subtle these days in westernised economies. We also find it in normal work practices. It is not until the practice becomes extreme that we start thinking about it. For instance, a person may be fired due to incompetence. That is fine you say, but many firings are due to Malevolent Managers getting rid of any opposition. All the senior manager has to say is that this person is incompetent. The label sticks and the person walks.

Think of office gossip. This seems innocuous, no one being hurt, but that is untrue, the subject of the gossip is usually not present when the talking happens. There may be a funny story to repeat, but nevertheless it is hurtful. The test to see if it is hurtful is to imagine the subject being present. Would that person like this story repeated to all and sundry? How would the listeners feel if the subject was present? Uncomfortable? Well, that means that it is emotionally violent. It is derogatory, vicious and puts the subject in a poor light. This is not normal to us as human beings as basically we are non-violent. We have become so used to these events that we do not see the violent action.

Many jokes are highly derogatory to some sections of society. Remember the 'Englishman, Irishman and Scotsman' jokes? Wherever you are in this world, there are similar jokes using a minority group as the base of the humour. If you are caught in this, you have to smile perhaps joining in the laughter so as to cover up the hurt that this brand of humour has caused. We have seen blonde jokes come and go which are against women as a whole, not just blondes. The 'How many ... do you need to change a lightbulb?' genre can be a dig at accountants, professionals, any group that you care to name and people laugh at the joke. It is hurtful therefore emotionally violent, and we as bystanders add credence to this by laughing with the joke teller and perhaps repeating it later on.

Men are particularly overt with their emotional violence. Usually it is isolating a group of people as the 'others' and a destructive humour is directed at that group. Persons can be singled out for this treatment, by harassing someone due to their apparent deficiencies. Apprentices have to go through traditional initiations as a way of joining the group. Women will do this behind a person's back and use such means as exclusion from 'The Group' as a form of emotional violence. They are more clandestine about their emotional violence, they use words, fashion, their standards of beauty to make the subject concerned isolated. They don't stick an individual's head down the toilet bowl, they use much more subtle means, such that the subject may well prefer the toilet bowl treatment. Some women use silence to exclude a person from the group. Unfortunately, I have done this myself and kept it up for 6 months. It was not a pretty sight, and I was wrong to have done it, but it was the only way I could think of making myself clear that I did not like the person concerned. I really wish I had been able to read this book when I was a teenager because I would have been less likely to have done that. See, we are not all perfect, are we?

Practical jokers are usually mean people. The subject of the joke is the target of some terrible, often violent action aimed at them, just because they are a different colour or have some other identifying difference. Pulling a chair away from under a person can be seen as hilarious, but little do the perpetrators realise that this can cause back injuries for the subject and complete humiliation to their psyche.

In the office, the Mediocre Managers are very subtle about their jokes, usually confining their humour to small groups or when away from the office, perhaps with after-hours drinks. They are the masters of office politics. They are the schemers who have worked out how to climb up the hierarchy based on who you know rather than what you know. When their activity is spotted by others they will receive derogatory labels. If you see this, and you know that this manager is true to that behaviour, then you have a Malevolent Manager on your hands, and you have to stay clear.

Mediocre Managers also wear the mask of good stewardship. Their credentials will be impeccable. Goffman observed that if the manager concerned is male, tall, and with Hollywood looks, then people will believe that this person is excellent at his job, when in fact he is not, he is only excellent at looking the part. Tyrant Managers do not have to rely on their looks, many are downright ugly, but as we live in fear of them, they do not need to have this factor playing for them.

The Fraudsters will want to look the part too, and indeed great effort is undertaken by the Arrogant Fraudster to look successful. The Likeable Fraudster will do this by adding many other features like free drinks, jollies such as conferences and other enticements to get the staff to do what he or she wants. One Mediocre Manager who was in my study constantly asked his cronies if he looked all right, was his tie straight and so on. Image is very important to the Mediocre, he or she knows that people judge on looks, so they take great care to conform to what is expected of the managerial style, with their hair, their clothes and so on. If green hair was part of the managerial look, they would be dying their hair accordingly.

Use of expert power and referent power by Malevolent Managers

In terms of using power, we know that the other managerial types of Executive Impression Management will use particularly expert power and referent power (French and Raven, 1960). The Arrogant Fraudster uses his expertise to be listened to and ensure that his advice and himself go upwards. The Tyrant has no need of expert power at all, his only expertise is that he has discovered how to make people go in fear of him, and that is all he needs. Media Tycoons are very good examples of this. They often have no skill whatsoever but are able to hire the expertise and make those people do their work under threat of being sacked or demoted, which is usually the worse threat of all as it means a public denigration of their expertise. Both types are concerned with looking and being successful. This is part of their expertise power. Probably there will be geeks who despise the suits who are of this type and will not conform, but even then, they will talk like an expert, which excludes most of us, and is also a part of their mask of expert power. For instance, a hacker who has defrauded millions still wants recognition from his own community. And we know that graffiti artists want the acknowledgement of being successful urban warriors, which is why they put their tag on their images, otherwise they would not bother.

Being an expert is fundamental to the fraud committed by Arrogant Fraudsters, whereas becoming a monopoly provider of information for instance, attributes total media expertise to the Tyrants. They crave power, they look the part of success, they act it, yet want more and more of it. This internal drive is hard to understand, but probably has its roots in early childhood trauma or even yet to be discovered bio-chemical imbalances in the brain. Tyrants and Arrogant Fraudsters are similar, it's just that the Tyrant is open with his machinations, his desires are clear, yet his plans may change at a moment's notice, but it is all about wanting to be number one in his or her area of expertise.

The complete opposite to these two types are the managers who use the Likeable Fraudster's and the Mediocre Manager's Executive Impression Management, who rely on referent power. This means that they induce people to like them so that they can manipulate them. I described this power earlier as inferior, as 'under' someone, as opposed to power 'over' someone. Both types of manager will develop groups of cronies around them, others are excluded from the glow of power that is bestowed upon the in-group. The manipulation is so subtle that it may not be seen as such, they use other guises such as being a mentor to a protégé – which is basically favouritism if no one else is offered similar treatment. They groom their favourite to be their backup when times are hard or their aims are thwarted. This is because they have seen that their climb up the hierarchy relies on everyone agreeing that the manager is a good one. Both Likeables and Mediocres deliberately use this as a tool of promotion of self to others. I am sure that some of you would have heard this in one form or another: 'Sorry, must go, have another long (substitute other deprecating words here) mentoring session with Joe.' Look into what is being said, and if you find disrespect, you have a Mediocre Manager talking to you.

One outcome of this behaviour is that Likeable Fraudsters and Mediocre Managers are promoted up the ladder quickly, as this practice relies strongly on similar managers in the system who play the same game. They end up in positions far beyond their expertise and have become the basis of what is known as the Peter Principle (Peter, 1969) whose author, a management radical, humoursly noted that managers rise to their level of incompetence. A rather sad commentary on management in fact.

Whereas we have no hard figures to work out how many Mediocre Managers there are in our society, I have made a guesstimate based on some evidence that indicates that at least 65 per cent of managers are Mediocres. Using random-based studies to infer the number of these managers is fraught with danger as we are talking here about social science, not natural science. The criterion of randomness as the basis of inference is impossible to meet in the social sciences. The only way that this can be measured is by taking a census of all managers, then my statement could be proved right or wrong. An impossible feat it may seem, but it may be necessary one day when the natural resources of our world have diminished to a critical danger point. As a world citizen, I would want to know that our dwindling resources are being looked after by responsible managers and not squandered in imperfect marketplaces by irresponsible management, as they so blatantly are today.

Our heritage of management

This critical role of management takes us right back to the beginnings of management about 8,000 years ago, when we transferred grain-keeping from individual households to large community stores. We needed responsible managers then to look after our food stores, as much as we will do in the future. Our basic human needs mean we must have food, drinking water and shelter, and we are beginning to see that these three criteria are already being threatened. Let's look more closely at these three requirements.

I live in Australia where water is at critical levels, I used to live in Canada, which has the world's largest water resources; in addition to the Great Lakes, the country currently has a further 31,000 largely unpolluted freshwater lakes. It might easily be possible to build a pipeline from Canada to Australia to ensure that Australia has enough water to survive. Apart from huge technical challenges, this sort of husbanding of resources is vital to the human race. Why not build a pipeline?

Food is wasted to an enormous extent, not only at point of production and transportation but in our shops and our fridges. We eat food that is bad for us in the long term, laced with sugars and fats, produced by multinationals for profit. Yet they are no better than the tobacco industry in that they are prioritising profit levels over health to the extent that we now see rising rates of obesity and diabetes in the Western world, and sadly this is also emerging in the developing countries like Indonesia. As these poisoned people become sick they take up resources in the medical sector through no fault of their own, and their care puts pressure on doctors and nurses who are diverted from other patients.

With housing, it is similar. The banks and financial institutions have driven market forces so high levels of interest and demands for high-percentage deposits have impacted many countries. Already in many countries we have housing that is too expensive for the next generation to buy. This is true in Australia, the United States, and the UK, and becoming a fact in Europe as well as China and India. Housing is at critical levels too. In the Third World a shack is a luxury, and many people are forced to live with their parents in multi-households. I have seen three households living in one room in northern Bali, hidden from the tourist gaze, which is not a lot of fun in the rainy season. Many countries do not have social housing either, so slums expand on fertile land and many people die early deaths due to the spread of hunger and disease.

These comments are from the point of view of managing our resources. It is 2018 as I write; what will my grandchildren face in 30 years' time? What sort of future can we give to people on this planet? Only well managed sustainable resources will work for us in the long term. What we faced in Neolithic times is what is facing us now. Who will manage? And will they be responsible stewards? So far, the record is not good, with more Malevolent Managers gaining control.

That means that current industry, business, public and social services are more likely to be operating at sub-optimal levels right now. Wastage and inefficiencies are a big problem in production and manufacturing, storing our own refuse is a major problem for many countries. We are exhorted to buy the latest fridge or car, and the ones that we buy have built in obsolescence. The question is why? And the answer is that Malevolent Managers want you to buy another car, and soon at that. Media tycoons do not want free speech, the basis of our democracies, they wish to control all parts of the media. This is not down to governments or agencies, it is down to management to be responsible in their jobs, and the Malevolent Managers currently systematically ruining our world for their short term gain of power and control. To take this premise to its logical end, it means that we will all be deceived and manipulated into a desolate world. Wars are not made by despots and maniacs, they are made by managers in their armed forces and in guerrilla groups. Armed forces are managed. Even terrorists are managed. It is time to tell the world that from our side at least, management has to own up to its malevolence.

On a recent trip to Central America I was appalled at the devastation that overcame the Mayan and other civilisations whch was basically due to total mismanagement of resources. At Chichen-Itza the capital of Maya culture, human sacrifice was the order of the day at each ceremony. After the still pumping heart was taken out of the victim, his or her body was thrown down the well from which Chichen Itza took its name. In doing so, they compromised their only water resource in a limestone karst plateau, and its 25,000 inhabitants had to rely on the Rain God to provide more water. This became unsustainable by the tenth century, and in order to survive people moved away to find sources of water and the civilisation imploded. The rise of their civilisation had been based on the maize plant, and they learnt to produce far more than they needed, and maize stores with their managers arose, just as they had done in the Fertile Crescent in the Middle East. One has to wonder what might have caused the similar endings that befall all known civilisations. My bet is on the Malevolent Managers and their use of increasingly unsustainable practices. And despite being the world's biggest optimist, I am certain that at some point we will end up the same if we do not change our ways.

So the question must be asked, 'What would Respectful Managers do with our three areas of need?' Simply, the answer is that they would ensure that everyone has access to clean water everywhere. Food producers would be more regulated to produce healthy products and clean up food fraud. Housing costs would be adjusted to more sensible levels, with fewer palaces and more social housing, and even free housing for the homeless. Sounds utopian, I agree but the thing about this view is that it is possible.

Could we expect peace and no wars? Well, the answer is a resounding yes. A Respectful Manager would walk away from war machines and related services. Wars and violence run counter to our basic human nature. Before 8,000 years ago, there is extremely little archaeological evidence to point to humans making warfare. So rare in fact, that the few skeletons that have been found with head wounds suggest that they may have been the result of accidents while hunting, not warfare. In fact, a hypothesis put forward by Faria (2015) explains holes in the head as caused by trepanning, the result of early surgery. It is only very recently that we have turned into warring societies.

We are not intelligent apes hitting each other with sticks. Therefore, violence is genetically primed within us. Eight thousand years is only 267 generations ago. We cannot make such a significant change in our DNA that quickly. No-one has put an anger gene into our bodies. However, what can change quickly is our behaviour when we are told that we have to be like this or we will starve otherwise. Therefore, it is back to food husbandry again. If we can share our resources with others then we will not have wars. Nevertheless, we have been made to feel that others will steal from us that which is rightfully ours. Famines come and go, but the western world retains its abundance of food. It would be very embarrassing to meet up with a long lost tribe to explain that we have fights over our food with others. Such tribes always ensure that their people have food. And when a traveller comes she will be given hospitality and share their food.

In the media lost tribes are portrayed as being warlike, but in fact, there are many more peoples who live in peace and honour others who arrive. As these tribes do not make good television we are not exposed to their ways of making peace in their natural environments. That's why it was such a shock to me when talking to the indigenous people in northern Bali to learn that they have no protracted conflict: they resolve issues immediately and fairly, so there are no ongoing grudges between individuals. Their workplaces are calm, their work is that of natural food producers.

For us, we have to address what we are doing. It is too easy to put the blame on the government and its generals. It is we who allow this to happen, as we are hoodwinked into thinking that we must defend ourselves, or assist others to win wars. The killing will never stop until we all understand that we must be respectful to each other's needs, and that sensible solutions can be found with reasonable outcomes for all. A Malevolent Manager is incapable of doing that. A Respectful Manager can, and does it as much as possible within her sphere of influence.

In hostage negotiations, mediators are trained to make the hostage taker understand that they comprehend their situation and are sympathetic to it. In business negotiations, Respectful Managers take a similar route. They put themselves in the other party's shoes and that gives them a sensitivity to the demands being made, no matter how extreme they may be. Treating others honourably is part of a Respectful Manager's make up. They may not like the individual they are dealing with, and totally disagree with their actions, but they will always treat them with respect.

How to treat a Malevolent Manager with respect

Many people ask me how to do this, especially with someone that they cannot tolerate. The only way to do this is by using compassion. Buddhist monks use compassion and so do I. It is the best way to live in this world with so much stress and pain suffered by many at the hands of a few. It changes anger, which is typified by intolerance, to respect. Saying it lightly, that you now respect this person, will not work. You have to have a deep understanding of what is happening. You must be motivated to change anger into something far softer, and more respectful.

Many people cannot give up their anger when it is actually in their best interests to do so. They cling on to it like a log in a lake of polluted water. Slowly they drown by taking in the pollution, and never reach the safety and comfort of dry land. It is an awful process to see, and you know you are witnessing when the individual says things like: 'I can try and forget those things, but I cannot ever forgive.' These statements are actual statements of hate. True forgiveness is arriving at a place of serenity about the past, something that is not often seen in the workplace. Grudges are kept and fester in the back rooms of the mind, anger grows and the person is more and more infected with a disease that they can turn around quite easily. The more the brain embraces the same activity as anger, the more neurons connect to that pathway and it becomes harder and harder to break and create new neural pathways (Norman Doidge explains this well in his 2007 book about the plasticity of the brain) of respect.

You can try and do this on your own, but others may need intensive help in the form of counselling from someone they trust. What you do is to sit down in a quiet place, preferably outside, but don't worry if you cannot do that. Quiet and calm is required for you to think uninterruptedly. Go through what has been said and done in the past by this person. Acknowledge that anyone in their position would feel the same. Think of other people who have gone through similar experiences and their reactions will be similar to yours. There is nothing new under the sun regarding people's maltreatment of others. Your reaction of anger is valid. No one should have to be treated in this manner.

Using compassion

Once these steps of acknowledgement and validation have taken place, then think about this person in depth. There must be something that you find that you can respect. The most awful and terrifying people who have walked this Earth always have something that can be respected. Let me give you an example. I personally do not like the idea of duck hunting. If I came across a manager who is a duck hunter I think I would be upset to know that this person will kill ducks, and does so regularly. I would not be able to say anything to him in the workplace and would have to put up with his stories of his kills. The anger inside me would build: how could I trust someone who willingly kills wild ducks? But there is one thing in his favour that I can latch onto. Most duck hunters fund protection of wild natural areas for their ducks to fly to, and in the right season can go out and shoot them. Such an example is 'Ducks Unlimited' a non-profit organisation in the United States that protects duck habitats, educates on how to keep wetlands from drying out, and so on. This means that the sport is continued, but a lot more ducks are living today (verified through Ducks Unlimited surveys) than there were 70 years ago. There is a flow on from this research into the increase in beaver populations who make wetlands through their dams and logging, other animals and insects thrive, retaining a diversity that could have so easily been lost. As you can see, there is always something that you can find, no matter how small to latch onto and praise the person's humanity. This journey of the mind is very similar to the saying that in each cloud there is always a silver lining. Finding that silver is hard when you are suffering, but it will always be there, I can guarantee it.

One of the Tyrant Managers that I have worked with was a detestable man in my eyes. I knew that his behaviour, as much as it was abhorrent, was probably due to a spoilt childhood. I didn't have any evidence, but the way he acted was just like a spoilt child who could not do a public tantrum. He was in his sixties and learnt that there were better ways to get what he wanted, and slowly he became labelled as a 'difficult' manager. And no one wanted to work with him for this reason. It was only on focussing on what he may have to offer me in terms of being a CEO of a large organisation that I kept sane and did not sink into anger. I knew that somewhere inside him, he could teach me the skills of large organisational management, which was my goal at the time. Finally, my body wore out and I nearly died twice through a respiratory illness and had to resign due to ill health. A couple of years later he died. There were many people at his funeral apparently, but I knew he had no real friends as he alienated anyone who was near to him. Before his death, I had to get into a stage of true forgiveness of his behaviour to me, so that I could survive and learn from what he had given me – a working example of a Tyrant, so when I came across co-workers in my research saying the same words, I recognised what we were dealing with. If I had only Respectful Managers in my career, perhaps I would have never believed that Tyrants existed! The lessons that I learnt from him have helped many managers with whom I have worked since. Not quite the skills I was looking for, but I learnt a far better and more comprehensive lesson than what I asked for at the time.

Compassion gives us a way through the suffering that befalls us in the workplace. Having compassion for your difficult manager or co-worker is the only way out from anger. Most people try alcohol or other drugs to try to forget their anger. Some take it out on 'safe' (read: unable to fight back) members of their family or their own co-workers. Others try to repress their feelings and one day the emotion spills out through their body breaking down with the stress of suppression, or they just die early through suicide. If you are suffering right now with anger, believe me, it must be dealt with quickly as it is like acid dissolving your brain. Anger eats away your reasoning powers as everything becomes clouded and eats away at those ties with family and friends. You may know the feeling of talking with someone, and all they talk about is the same old stuff which you have heard many times before. It is the repetition which points to the anger. Venting once or twice is a healthy way to divest yourself of a negative emotion but repeating it over and over again to anyone who crosses your path is bald anger.

From my examples above, I can now live with duck hunters and Tyrant Managers; their activities will not affect me, even though I highly disapprove of their behaviour. Many managers have learnt from me that there is a way of living through Malevolent Managers' antics by using compassion. If you are affected, then learn to use it. Toleration is a basic human right. Everyone wishes to be accepted or at least be tolerated. This means laying down our arms, a true act of surrendering to our common humanity. We cannot use violence to achieve toleration. Only compassion can do that.

A Respectful Manager understands the meaning of compassion. This is why he is able to talk to the office cleaner in the same way as he does to his chief executive officer. Although it is often hidden in the workplace, just take some time to see who offers compassion around you. HR managers are meant to have this, but many are there to enforce low wages and reduce industrial action rather than genuinely offering a true compassionate service to employees. That is why I suggest that staff should avail themselves of employee assistance programs if they are offered by the company. A trained counsellor is the best person to speak to about problems. It keeps the complaints away from the workplace and prevents them backfiring on the worker and also gives time for them to devise a workable solution. Often the plan has to be to find another job elsewhere and in order not to leap from the frying pan into the fire, to find a Respectful Manager to work with. They are the only ones who will give you the respect that you deserve.

This does not mean that you should spend your time with your Respectful Manager giving a long list of complaints about your work. He is trusting you to resolve them in the best way possible. Most Respectful Managers work long hours to get the business moving quicker. It is best to use your time wisely as she will always listen to you when she has the time.

I had a Respectful Manager once ask me about her employees; some she liked very much and others were only there plodding away until their retirement. She wondered if indeed she was a Respectful Manager. I asked a few questions about her relationships with her co-workers, and she said yes, there were friends that she had made in her workplace, but she was never intolerant of the others. She found them hard to work with, however; she tolerated their ways, but looked forward to the day when at last they would retire and everyone would be relieved. Some workplaces are stuck with employees that others hired and who are not as productive as they could be. In some countries it is illegal to fire an employee, which is a good thing in many ways, but it does point to the fact that these workplaces will be less productive. A Respectful Manager may organise and assign duties to the more able, or tactfully suggest more productive ways to assist the organisation. One such manager told me that after a problem employee declared that every day he was exhausted, he suggested a career move for that person as obviously where he was right now was not meeting his personal needs. Again, this was done with maximum sensitivity and not to dehumanise the individual.

Working with people with disabilities is an area that Malevolent Managers detest. These employees are seen as a drain on the company's resources. Similarly, with affirmative action programs, they feel that they are forced to take on a 'table decoration' in the board room when governments legislate for gender equality at senior level. Only Respectful Managers will see that these are very important issues as they bring diversity to the workforce and give more diverse answers to what previously might have appeared to be intractable problems. Barring a person with a disability from the workplace is a racist crime in my view; every workplace can be designed around the individual. At one organisation we had a blind person on reception. This was joked about behind his back, but a manager stood up for him and asked: 'Why not?' This soon sent the Malevolent Managers packing, but the innuendoes were still there. A Respectful Manager can see their way through such problems and even assist the person further with training and development – which is their one big characteristic that they give every co-worker the benefit of.

If you are not being considered for further training and development after several years have passed, your seemingly Respectful Manager is in fact a Malevolent Manager. Many co-workers don't latch on to this at first, as many of us like to think the best of a situation when we first enter the workplace. The flush of a new job, learning who is who, trying your best, is all part of the induction process that goes with any new job. It would be silly to suggest that any training and development would take place immediately, unless you are drafted in specifically, so staying in situ and watching what is going on is for many a wise move, until with the passing of time nothing comes their way at all.

It must be said that the co-workers in my study liked their Respectful Managers very much. But they felt equal to their manager, even if they were several rungs down the ladder. This may look like referent power, but it is not. It is an outcome of respectful behaviour, it is not a practice of grooming a person for the manager's own purposes. There is no favouritism, cronyism or in-group with a Respectful Manager.

The Likeable Fraudster and the Mediocre Manager figure out which of their co-workers are trustworthy – this is not a quick assessment and it may take a few months of background chat with others who know the individual concerned. The checking produces information that can be used for flattery when the time comes. Sometimes mistakes are made by these managers, and a respectful person becomes the appointed favourite, but as soon as the reality becomes evident, the manager will drop them instantly, leaving a very bemused and confused co-worker who wonders what has happened to them. One co-worker talked about her own experience with this, which left her even more cynical about her organisation which allowed this type of behaviour. Her experience gave me the interesting insight that Mediocre Managers will apologise if it is politically expedient to do so, when he offered her such an apology. Luckily, she was astute enough to see through it, as his behaviour did not change one iota.

Mediocre Managers also use favouritism once they have gained the co-worker's trust. This is a terrific device as the favourite becomes the preferred candidate for any promotion, and in return will do anything that is required. The problem with being the favourite is that despite the power that is conferred on them, tomorrow things can be entirely different depending on the political landscape of the organisation. The princeling can be deposed at a moment's notice, depending entirely on their manager's whim.

Talking of princes, if you have read Machiavelli's (1532) work on how to be a prince (for prince, read substitute manager) you will have discovered for yourself the way to be a Mediocre Manager. Typically, they are kind to your face while behind your back they will demonise you. A more modern-day example would be the innumerable politicians who fall into this bracket. You are able to spot the behaviour as you see them quickly changing allegiances and policies in order to stay on top. What people do not understand is that this is the norm in workplaces around the world and causes untold misery.

However, as stated before, the two fundamental factors are that the manager should be consistent in all of the walks and talks, and treats you like an equal, despite what is said to the contrary. We know that all disguises crack over time, notwithstanding their wearer's efforts. Even the masters of disguise will have little odd things appear that should, but often do not, have people questioning the integrity of that manager. The delusion is hard to crack, which is why I advise people to leave rather than fight, as you will end up the loser because there is less power in your position as compared to the manager concerned.

Enticements

Malevolent Managers offer all sorts of enticements to their co-workers. More often than not these are not laid on a foundation of truth or even intentions. In my study, I found that co-workers were even offered partnerships, as well as being able to go to conferences and other goodies. But when the time came, all the carrots came to nought. Certainly, all promises can be broken in the Malevolent Manager's eyes. If it is not going to assist his own personal goals of power and control, then any promise is broken.

There is a huge difference in inspiring co-workers and yet the business plans do not work out, and sloppy management with the same business plan result. With the Respectful Manager, this means that everyone is involved in the global vision and can see where the organisation is going, and also their own future. However, market forces can easily change, new entrants to the market may be unseen as well as advances in technology. The rough seas of entrepreneurship are mostly unforecastable and it is impossible to predict exactly where a company is going and how well it will fare. However, the difference with a Respectful Manager is that he or she will do all that is possible to assist everyone to survive. There may be casualties, but again every opportunity to assist the co-worker is taken. With malevolent management you will see managers jumping overboard to more 'secure' jobs. They will make scapegoats of anyone in the organisation who has predicted the poor outcome. In other words, they have to blame othes. It has nothing to do with themselves.

You can always spot the Respectful Manager in organisational change. They are the ones who try to protect their team and if not allowed to, they will try to help those people in the best ways that they can. They may spend time helping them in a job search, giving honest references. They may also use their own contacts to find work for the employee. I have even seen ousted workers receiving re-training and outplacement packages for workers who are below the normal level for receiving such benefits in finding work. Unions like working with such managers as they realise that their members will not be laid off without support. Often the Respectful Manager will liaise with unions to discuss best strategies for their members. But Malevolent Managers will only do this if they are forced to. The co-workers that are about to be retrenched are seen as a problem to get rid of immediately, and then their focus can return to their own ambitions.

As Malevolent Managers help other Malevolent Managers, they are deeply engaged in mutual backscratching. This is often how top jobs are handed out, also directorships and awards. They are transactional in intent. If the action taken is not repaid then that individual is not rewarded any further, and usually is penalised for not doing what is considered by these managers as the right thing. If the recipient returns the favour not only once but twice, this is seen as ingratiating by the superior manager. There are quite strict but unsaid rules that govern these actions and they are all part of the repertoire of a Malevolent Manager. If the lower manager expects certain accolades and they are not given, then fury can be unleashed at whomever has spoilt the game. It is a matter of give and take. Receive and be delighted in your good fortune, even though you may not have ever deserved it.

I quite like reading the honours lists that are handed out in Australia and the UK. Among the saints there are many who truly do not deserve such acclaim but receive it because they are well entrenched in the system. When Anthony said: 'I have come to bury Caesar, not to praise him' it was seen as treacherous, as the expectation, which Shakespeare knew well, was that to inter an emperor meant doing this with honour, and to not do so was the ultimate betrayal.

Similarly, looking at promotions in organisations, co-workers can estimate if the promotion was deserved, and if it was not, then a Malevolent Manager has received it from the promotion giver, another Malevolent Manager. The recipients of such promotions do not mind standing out like this in an organisation; both sides think that this does not expose their malevolence, but it does. If you are in an organisation and wish to delve into whether a promotion was deserved or not, just send out a questionnaire that is to be responded to anonymously, and you will hear the truth from co-workers. I have witnessed an individual rise from the lowest level to almost the top, by sheer transactional promotions over a number of years. The whole organisation was aware of this, but could do no more than shrug its shoulders and carry on with their work, as it would have been useless to complain to the tyrant boss. The recipient of course, was resolutely faithful to him, no matter what was said or done that was unethical or shady. Thus, another stalwart was added to the boss's platform.

Sticks

The following has happened to me several times, so I feel that you must understand this form of malevolence. Sometimes the CEO needs to interfere with a recruitment to ensure that his favourite will win, but by sheer numbers a selection panel may go against his wishes and choose the better candidate. The internal one being well known to lack ability and the intended favourite having fewer skills and experience that could be applied to the position. When an outside candidate wins the position, the CEO is silently spitting bullets, but prepares to undermine them on day 1 of the candidate's entry into the organisation. The failed manager then commences a stealth campaign with the intention of destabilising the new manager, which proceeds over many months. However, to seem not to be a spoiler, the failed manager has to be obsequious to the new intake, and yet undermine every move the new manager makes. What interested me was that the examples that I came across did such amazing pieces of back-stabbing that they were never held accountable. Not one observer would put up their hand and ask the relevant question as to the power of the failure and the clandestine support received by the boss.

Secrets are another way to control these underling Malevolent Managers. The senior manager goes about finding out details of every organisational activity, for example checking corporate credit card expenses, so that they can gain knowledge to use to their advantage. A vast corporate illicit knowledge is accumulated which is available to be used in future whenever the subordinate manager falls out of line. This again is part of the transactional nature of these Malevolent Managers.

Respectful Managers do not engage in any of this type of activity. They are not driven by personal gain of power and control, they are there to do a job and to do it well. They are aware however, of what is going on, and often are forced to keep quiet to continue their work without attracting trouble.

The Respectful Manager does not use these types of controls on their co-workers. They are not transactional as the Malevolent Managers are. The researchers Avolio and Bass (1999), who put the theory together of transactional versus transformational leaders, pointed out that the transactional manager does not make a very good leader. This is due to their participation in behaviour with others if there is a reward in it for them. They also make lazy leaders as they leave everyone to do their job, and only intervene if there is an exception to the rules of the organisation. These behaviours describe the Mediocre Manager very well. As we know from Executive Impression Management theory, they will do very little that is out of step and prefer to hold to the status quo. When they become CEOs or heads of organisations, they are not noteworthy for being creative. They will become bureaucratic, watching to see if anyone breaks the rules. This behaviour of course, ensures that their self-built castles on sand will not be eroded by the seas of innovation and change. And as it keeps everyone in line, then life is easy and they can bask in the sunshine of easy rewards and favours and a luxurious retirement.

The Respectful Manager, however, exhibits many of the transformational leader's characteristics of having charisma, inspiration, intellectual stimulation and individualised consideration. Not all Respectful Managers will become leaders; they may feel that this should be left to others. They certainly show to co-workers that they have individual consideration for them, and they train and develop them where agreed, which also touches on intellectual stimulation and inspiration.

Malice

I have witnessed many episodes of malice that is exhibited where the Malevolent Manager can get away with it, even years after an episode has been long forgotten by others. One example was after a manager left employment to seek better opportunities and found that every job offer was sabotaged by the former employer upon reference checking. Malice can be seen in other situations, making the manager feeling left out, stranded without any support from the board or senior managers. Hostility can be seen with harsh emails, warnings given without fair adjudication. Redundancies of positions in which employees have been whistleblowers are unfair dismissals and usually down to sheer malice on the manager's part. Company cars have been reported missing to the police, another trick in their books, as well as spreading wicked rumours about the manager in question that purport to give the 'real' reason behind their departure.

Again, no Respectful Manager would ever think about inflicting these malicious tricks on their co-workers. Even when co-workers do not see eye to eye with their manager, the co-worker will leave in the certain knowledge that the Respectful Manager will give a reference, as they understand that the individual concerned still needs a job. The way a Respectful Manager will give information is that it will be truthful, although the reference may be shorter than usual.

Goffman's marks of good character

The Respectful Manager conforms to Goffman's properties of good character (1967), of courage, gameness, integrity, gallantry, and composure. He wrote these words in the 1960s and the language is different today. Courage in the workplace allows individuals to face great risk of harm. For instance, we know about heroism and such acts, but in work terms it may be taking a risk with new strategies. Here we know that the marketplace is not a fair place to work, governments issue tariffs, and certain firms may be designated as tariff free. It creates unfair advantages to favoured industries. Other factors can be taking on new ideas in organisational change. To drive programs of non-violence in the workplace takes great courage as, if the business has the typical profile of Executive Impression Management types, then about 80 per cent of the present management must undergo great personal changes or be sacked. A Respectful

Manager will do this. They understand the risk of failure, but they also believe that the objectives are worth fighting for.

This leads onto gameness, which means that a manager will achieve goals no matter the setbacks. This points out a characteristic of the Respectful Managers who have the ability to use 'work arounds' and innovate as they go along. This is a talent that Malevolent Managers do not possess and rely on others to do this. Integrity has been covered earlier in Chapter 3, but it also includes the ability to resist temptation, particularly when faced with great gains and little accountability.

The Respectful Manager is simply unable to commit fraud; it is impossible for them, due to their internal moral fabric. I once had the opportunity to defraud an organisation of millions of dollars, but never did, as I just could not do it. If you have an inner moral compass, you do not have 'opportunities', they are just loopholes in the system, and must be reported and closed to stop others availing themselves of such openings. Self-discipline is part of the moral code of a Respectful Manager, and it is this which reinforces the integrity of the manager, who will not succumb to temptation as it is not on their radar.

Another characteristic is gallantry, which in many ways is like heroism. I am not referring to opening doors for women or people in wheelchairs, it is about knowing that the game may be lost but continuing even at a cost to yourself. A man jumping into a river to save a dog is truly gallant. The rushing river might be dangerous, particularly if the man is a poor swimmer, but if successful, it is one of those unsung acts that happen daily in our world. Within the workplace it is unacknowledged outside of the organisation, but everyone inside knows the truth of what happened. Let me give you an example. One respondent to my study mentioned that her boss always worked extra long hours to avoid losing a very awkward customer. The customer represented over one-third of the company's earnings. When eventually, despite everything, the customer was enticed away by another firm, that meant for the staff that there would be no bonus that year. Come the end of the year, the boss gave out bonuses, albeit small ones, and refused to take one himself. He put a huge effort into trying to keep the client; it failed, but he ensured that his staff would not lose out completely. That is real gallantry in the workplace.

Finally, Goffman thought that composure was indeed a fundamental characteristic of a good person. Being calm in dangerous situations is a great asset, as the Respectful Manager is able to draw people's attention to how to get out of the crisis that faces them, rather than focussing on the danger at hand. Many people in my study talked about composure on the part of the fraudsters, but that is to do with the mask that the fraudster is wearing to deceive others. This will eventually crack and expose the fraudster given enough time. However, the composure that Goffman refers to is more about keeping one's cool in a crisis, thus giving others the chance to think clearly and move in the right direction.

Risk Management

Panic is easily caught by others and creates more harm than good. We know from car accidents, air crashes, or buildings catching fire, that people do not act reasonably when faced with enormous odds against survival. But a few do; they show calmness with the presence of mind to think rationally through the crisis. The performance in impression management terms is one of dignity and stage confidence, which does not stress others. To me this is an essential part of risk management, and is reflected when assigning a Respectful Manager who becomes the designated leader when disaster strikes. In our hierarchies in organisations these positions are meant to be held by senior management, but quite often they haven't a clue as to what to do. Disaster recovery is an important part of leadership in my view, but for many it is not. We have witnessed in floods and fires that those companies with an off-site disaster recovery unit are back in business more or less immediately. I would rather my boss be a Respectful Manager, as then I would be satisfied that my welfare is taken seriously and that there will be a strong chance of survival as the scenarios are thought about and planned for in advance. A Malevolent Manager would only think about himself and subsequently there will be less of his time available for others.

Before the World Trade Center attacks of 11 September 2001, Rick Recorla, a security director with Morgan Stanley, whose offices were on higher floors in WTC Tower 2 than where the planes struck, had previously insisted on fire evacuation drills being carried out every 3 months. This meant the survival of more than 2,600 people, as the disaster was actually planned for. Recorla was convinced that the World Trade Center would be attacked after the 1993 truck bombing in the basement. Thanks to Recorla's efforts only seven of their office workers were lost (unfortunately Recorla was too), whilst others were told to stay at their stations or went to close down their computers, go to the toilet, and other incidental activities, before moving to the stairs to evacuate – losing vital seconds and possibly their lives. A total of 2,606 lives were lost in the attack and the subsequent implosion of both towers. It is not their fault that they died, but the fault of both their management that did not care enough for their staff in disaster situations, and also the risk management aspect of the buildings' design.

On a similar note, aircraft evacuations centre on a crucial 90 second period immediately after a crash. This is because enough safety people have gone through the remains of so many crashes and come to understand that this is the critical period. If you don't get out within 90 seconds you are unlikely to make it at all. I cannot say that all airlines run without malevolent management, but what I am saying is that there are enough Respectful Managers in place in accident review boards who have insisted that this regulation be followed by all airlines and staff be trained accordingly.

In the business world, we have seen stock market crashes with similar reactions, where people commit suicide. Also, when something major goes wrong with the enterprise, people have been known to run away and hide rather than face up to the consequences. A recent example of an awful tragedy was the Grenfell Tower fire in London in June 2017. It is estimated that 71 people died; and all those who survived lost their possessions as well as family and friends. The prime minister, Theresa May, attended a very strictly controlled, rapid visit to the site the next day, but met with criticism when she failed to meet with any residents. The queen and the leader of the parliamentary opposition showed her how it should be done on the following day, by meeting with the residents who had lost everything. Judging by her rushed, private visit, it would seem that the prime minister feared meeting the residents, almost that she had to do it like that in order to escape their wrath. Such disasters are unfortunately part of our life, but how you treat people is the mark of the composure that Goffman was talking about. Composure creates understanding of the event and allows us to convey our sincerity in actions that may be in fact be dangerous to ourselves.

Another example took place in Paris after the terrorist attack on the *Charlie Hebdo* newspaper offices in January 2015, when the French prime minister requested a minute's silence in parliament. After the 60 seconds had passed, a lone voice started singing the *Marseillaise*, the French national anthem. This one person turned an extremely sad moment to one of resoluteness as the whole National Assembly joined in. This sent a message very clearly to terrorists that such actions would not be tolerated and that France would stand firm. To emphasise how strong an effect this had on the French people it should be noted that the *Marseillaise* had not been sung in the National Assembly since the end of World War 1. That lone voice had the character which Goffman described so well, and by singing out confronted the terrorists head on. After the singing, the next piece of legislation that was passed was France upscaling its input into the ongoing Middle East war, where the jihadists who claimed responsibility for the *Charlie Hebdo* killings were active. Since then there have been several terrorist attacks claiming the lives of hundreds of people, yet France has not given in, and will remain steadfast for a long time. Do not confuse this example with nationalism and warmongering. It is not. The child that stands up for a bullied school boy or girl does the same thing. I am proud of my grandson who at the age of 7 demonstrated to the class bully that he is not to touch others. That shows much character in a little boy, who will hopefully grow up repeating such acts and not tolerate victimisation of innocents.

Usage of coercion

Respectful Managers do not use sticks on their co-workers. Ultimatums may be given but these will be part of an enterprise-wide phenomenon. Such acts, if said only to one person – 'I need this by Friday or you're fired' – are not done by Respectful Managers. This is coercion in a format that is outside a Respectful Manager's repertoire.

Apart from getting rid of co-workers who are in some way seen as working against their ambitions, the most prominent stick that Malevolent Managers will use is bullying. It comes in many forms and often the target does not realise that it is happening. They recognise that there is a problem, but again through the power of Executive Impression Management, do not see that it is bullying. If you suspect that your Respectful Manager is participating in such behaviour, then the manager concerned is not a Respectful Manager, more likely a Mediocre Manager who is disguising his real intentions.

Bullying styles of Malevolent Managers

This list is unfortunately long but enables people to identify what this behaviour truly represents. I use here the terminology of Non-Violent Communication (Rosenberg, 1998) so that the person that receives the aggression is referred to as the target. Using the discourse of victim or survivor denotes immense suffering, which indeed happens, but when you are in the situation, you will not recognise your symptoms of suffering, only that something is seriously wrong. By using the word target, it feels less emotional and more objective. Once you have identified that you are a target, then the other words will fit, thereby starting the process of healing, as the problem is recognised for what it actually is.

A Malevolent Manager's attitude to the target can be openly offensive, even using obscenities in front of others, or being wary, scheming in approach, outwardly passive-aggressive. Pushing the buttons within the organisation to maintain pressure on the target is often a used ploy. Coercion is achieved by intimation of job loss, or planning to push the target out, or to increase pressure on the target without it being too obvious. Either way the target's behaviour is being controlled. The target loses control of his own work, his or her style of working and timing.

It is important to the bullying manager that the target loses status, so humiliation is an overt way of doing this, while others will take credit for the target's work. This will include derogatory remarks about the target, and sabotaging and undermining him. The ridiculing happens openly but where the manager has his own clique, the ridicule will happen behind the target's back. Insults will fly from the managers, or damning with faint praise, a backward insult, leaving the target defenceless. Sometimes the target is openly yelled at with screaming abuse, while other managers will make abusive statements in a sarcastic way but never in front of the target.

Being constantly criticised, the target feels confused as to what is going on, and furthermore, on how to correct this. If it happens when the target is unaware, but everyone else knows what is going on, it leaves the target powerless to defend or correct the record. In meetings, the target's opinions are belittled. Usually participants of the meeting know what is going on, and some will feel embarrassed while others will feel righteous, that the criticism is justified. Exclusion by discussing certain topics before the meeting begins is often used. Typical for women to experience is the sports talk that takes place among male managers. I have been in meetings where this 'small talk' has taken 20–30 minutes, and then the items on the agenda are fleetingly addressed, with no time to discuss important issues.

The culture of drinking at meal times and after work is also part of the repertoire of bullying. It openly discriminates if the target is unable to meet after hours commitments, or is teetotal, or not part of the dominant male manager gang. Drinking then leads on to more risqué topics such as watching pornography back at the office or going to bars with strippers and so on. Co-workers are co-opted into this sort of behaviour to support the dominant position of the manager concerned, but what they are doing is essentially supporting the bullying culture. It must be said that the sin of omission is as great as the sin of commission, so the participants, even the reluctant ones, preserve the status quo.

The demands the bully makes of the target increase over time to the point that the target has to work much overtime – of course unpaid is preferable from the bully's point of view – to fulfil these unreasonable requests. *Karoshi* is the word that the Japanese use to describe this sequence of self-destruction under relentless stress from work. It is a well-known fact that working in excess of 60 hours a week leads to cardiac failure, inflammatory diseases and so on (Brotman et al., 2007). We do not have an equivalent word for this process in the English language, which to me is worthy of note, indicating that we do not recognise it or even care. The nearest we get to it is 'workaholism'. However, workaholism implies that the person happily throws himself into work and works such incredible hours that no one else sees him at evenings and on weekends. It is seen as a pattern of avoidance of social relationships. But the compliance of the workaholic may not be a happy one after all, just a person drowning in over-work. Moreover, judgements are made against such a person, that he is unable to delegate and so on. But the reality may be that here is a worker who is scared out of his wits by unreasonable management, just trying to keep his job.

The reality is, of course, that the workaholic co-worker is supporting a lazy manager, whether a Tyrant or Mediocre in Executive Impression Management terms. But the bullying manager cannot admit this to anyone, let alone to the target. There is no acknowledgement, in public or private. Quite the opposite occurs, where the output of the target is condemned as rubbish.

One exquisite form of bullying is to leave the target high and dry with no real duty statement. No direction is given in this type of abuse. The manager concerned is abrogating his responsibility of good stewardship, as the point is that every co-worker should know what to do and how to do it. Not giving any guidance leaves the target spinning, not knowing what is expected of them; and when it comes to performance evaluation time – if such a process exists in the organisation – the target only then finds out that he should have been doing other functions. In the study, one co-worker described how he was left alone to do his work in an office away from others in the open plan work area, and completely isolated from what he was meant to be doing. He then decided on a course of activity which was ultimately deemed wrong by the management. This allowed the bullying manager to say that the target was useless, did not take directions well, and other unjustified criticisms, when in fact that manager was himself responsible.

Feigning politeness or even friendship is another form of passive-aggressive manipulation. When the target finds out the truth, that the manager concerned actually dislikes him, then the target becomes much affected with lack of trust issues. We trust those around us to tell the truth and when it turns out to be a lie it is very damaging to the target. Also, co-workers of the target often know the truth but fail to warn him, and his trust of them is undermined as well.

One principle of torture is to disassociate the individual from his reality, by persuading him that his so-called friends are in fact enemies. We do this to each other in the workplace and what do so many do? Turn a blind eye to the psychological abuse that is perpetrated by Malevolent Managers. My advice to those who witness such acts is to take the target aside and tell him that the abuse is being witnessed and disliked by others. The sooner this is done, the less psychological harm there will be. If the behaviour is allowed to continue uninterrupted then as an individual you must take responsibility as you could have prevented it from escalating.

Many co-workers get stuck in their moral reasoning as to what to do in these situations; there is also fear that the same thing will happen to them. One way to minimise fear of the bullying manager is to tell the co-worker in a neutral place, one that is unlikely to be seen by others in the organisation. A cafe or a stroll in the park may be suitable, but it has to be done away from the workplace as the threat of someone overhearing is too great.

When the target knows the reality, there is going to be an emotional fallout. It is best to counsel evaluation first, collect evidence in emails, meetings and so on, and then a confrontation to the manager in the presence of senior management. If the situation is untenable for the target, it is better to undertake an out of hours job search immediately. Upon resignation, tell senior management, or the board, if appropriate, the reasons why you are leaving. This places the responsibility for the wrongful acts on those who should take action. It does not mean to say that they will, but they have duty of care towards their employees, to have a workplace that is not harmful to individuals. This includes emotional and psychological damage, which bullying always achieves.

One day I hope that legislation will be passed where such bullying in the workplace will be outlawed and punishments assigned accordingly. It would give Respectful Managers more clout in an organisation that is run by Malevolent Managers if the latter are breaking the law by tolerating such harmful behaviour. There are occupational health and safety laws for entire industries, and if it is found that an organisation has breached those laws penalties are imposed. If we can do that with issues of physical harm in the workplace then we can easily extend it to the emotional health of employees.

As in the old days, domestic violence was seen to be appropriate if it was committed inside the home and the victims were at fault for goading or nagging the perpetrator. Gradually, awareness of physical violence has put strong penalties in place for this. There is now a move to ensure that emotional violence is not tolerated by society and judges are handing out sentences to perpetrators on this point alone. In 2015 new legislation was put into place in the UK by which the domestic abuse definition was widened to include a pattern of threats, humiliation and intimidation. The offending partner can be facing a sentence of 5 years jail for doing so. The definition of domestic abuse is:

> abuse can include a pattern of threats, humiliation and intimidation, or behaviour such as stopping a partner socialising, controlling their social media accounts, surveillance through [software] apps or dictating what they wear.
> (UK Crown Prosecution Service, as reported by the Press Association, *Daily Telegraph*, 29 December 2015)

Eventually the same move, I hope, will be made regarding emotionally abusive behaviour in the workplace.

The Respectful Manager's role in cases of bullying is to protect the target from the Malevolent Manager's actions. A Respectful Manager does not let things slide unnoticed, he or she will proactively intervene, particularly if there is strong evidence to do so – which emphasises the importance of documenting evidence of the abuse. It is possible to see now the gallantry and courage of the Respectful Manager's character when in a situation like this.

Sadly, it is often the case that a so-called Respectful Manager turns out to be less than respectful and will want to save their own hide.

When I was being bullied by my CEO, and it eventually came to a showdown, the chairperson who was present at my final meeting just wrung his hands and said that there was nothing he could do. Those words still reverberate inside my head, because when you consider how much power a chairperson has over their CEO, the statement is laughable. At the time I thought it was unbelievable, particularly considering that he wanted me there to change the organisation in line with strategic goals, which I was already accomplishing. So, from being my ally and protector it was finally revealed that I had a Mediocre Manager on my hands in the chairperson's office. This breaking of fundamental trust was very damaging to me, and for years that particular act hurt very much. Considering that I had earlier gone through a recovery process about my feeling of rejection, stemming from my early separation from my mother, and that the hurt stayed for a long time, demonstrates the damage that can be caused by a loss of trust. Never underestimate how much devastation this causes in the name of organisational politics.

If a Respectful Manager had been there as chair, I would not have been discarded so lightly. This is because such people believe in the fundamental good in others, and such shenanigans would have been stopped. It takes bravery to stand up to a bullying CEO, but the right person could have done so. But it was not meant to be and I look back at this incident as an important lesson I learned, that Mediocres can disguise themselves as good and caring, but in the end will always sacrifice others as a pawn in the political game to meet their own needs of power and control.

This example demonstrates that there are many weak chairperons out there and that they take on a position only for the money and the prestige that it affords them. It also demonstrates that many a strategic plan is sabotaged by the very people that the plan has been put forward to change. Eventually in that situation the CEO was pensioned off and the chairperson was quickly replaced.

Bullying behaviours also include the use of organisational spies who report to the Malevolent Manager on the doings of the target. One CEO I know of played the unions against management and management against the unions. He was a master at it. I wonder to this day if the union ever suspected the double dealing that was going on. One senior manager that I know had his managers primed to hand over information on the credit card expenditures of a certain other manager. This may not seem to be a good example, but the reality is that if the action is underhanded then only a Malevolent Manager will be at the heart of it.

In my work of identifying Malevolent Managers, I recommend the spot audit. This uncovers all sorts of hidden expenditures such credit card payments, spending on what may be considered as self-promoting rather than for the good of the business. A Respectful Manager is always open to spot audits, but those who complain of them will usually have something to hide. Going through the conference budget is always an eye-opener as, if it is only a select few that attend, you can be assured that these are most likely favourites of the Malevolent Manager. Training is less of a carrot to offer his favourites as there is a dedicated outcome, but conferences, particularly those held in exotic locations, could be deemed as payments for services rendered, that is, for being a toady.

A Respectful Manager will never be outwardly angry with a person in the organisation. If he is angry, he knows that he has to deal with this emotion, rather than take it out on the person concerned. If a mistake is made, it is cause for correction, not for losing one's temper. If the manager suddenly heats up, then asks you to leave his office, then this is a good sign of someone getting their emotions under control. There is no storming into the workplace and tearing a person to shreds; there is a calm discussion about what went wrong, and how to put in place procedures to prevent it happening again. That is all.

If the person concerned repeats the error then serious action has to take place. There has to be an official warning, and if it happens again, then dismissal must occur. Seemingly soft-hearted bosses say that they cannot do that as the co-worker needs his job and so on. This is not the right response, as it only creates future errors. It is far better to investigate the reason, and job or no job, the person has to leave if it is committed again.

Some people have been exposed to their boss's temper tantrums, and this display of anger does unconsciously affect them. It is embarrassing for others to see, and the target feels diminished and hurt. Temper tantrums in an adult are an outward display of unresolved childhood issues, where this sort of behaviour used to incur rewards from the parent concerned. Tyrants are especially prone to this type of behaviour, while a Mediocre Manager knows to keep his temper under control and play the political game for his advancement. Usually the Mediocre Manager will let off steam in front of others, denigrating the person behind his back, with no right of reply. It is a nasty, dirty practice and those who witness it should walk away. Without an audience, the manager concerned will soon back down.

But there has to be a discussion about the error and its correction. It is important to consider impossible goals and whether the manager is micro-managing the target. These behaviours belong to the manager, and are not grounds for dismissal in a just world. If the demands are too high, then the manager is at fault, and if it is a case of micromanagement, then the manager has to learn to back off. Often a Malevolent Manager will use micro-management on his targets to get them to leave. This is never the case with a Respectful Manager.

If a person has to be dismissed, then it is done fairly and justly. There are no instant dismissals, although there may be instant suspension with or without pay, for the matter to be dealt with more care. An investigation may have to take place, or others need to be conferred with, but no one gets kicked out of the door within 15 minutes. That is the stuff of Tyrant Manager bullies. A suspension is a good process as it keeps the job open for the co-worker should he be deemed fit to return. The police and armed forces do this for good reason, as where the truth of the matter lies may not be apparent at first and only an inquiry can have the power to find out what really happened. Then if dismissal is truly deserved then it must take place, or else restitution work take place. Respectful Managers will always respect the individual even while not condoning his behaviour. And that is a real mark of a person who is not having to rely on the goodwill of others like the Malevolent Managers do. An enquiry can be set up while the person is on suspension, and with a due diligence process the matter can be resolved. In my lifetime's experience as an employment counsellor to many managers, it has always been awful to hear the horror stories of those who have been kicked out of organisations for very little reason. Summary dismissal is not something to be undertaken lightly, and Respectful Managers would never do it in normal circumstances. Even under immense pressure, the suspension process gives time for everyone to cool off and time is given later to review the situation.

One way a Mediocre Manager controls staff for his own needs is to send them off on activities that give the manager knowledge which is of value for himself and not others. Sometimes co-workers are assigned meaningless tasks as a way of moving the target sideways, particularly if the target is blocking his path to success. There are organisations that do not allow dismissals; in fact there are entire countries that also adhere to this practice, for instance China. In these cases moving someone sideways is therefore the only option in a large organisation. A Respectful Manager who does this would do it in the interest of the co-worker and not for himself. There may be, for example, opportunities for an individual to learn other tasks that are more suited to their needs.

If employees are needed for their specific expertise, they will be tolerated by the manager until the day that they are no longer of use to him. Tyrants will shout and scream their abuse, Mediocres will manipulate and pull the wool over people's eyes about the more subtle abuse that they inflict on their targets.

Mediocres, for example, will give meaningless tasks to such an employee and then say behind their back that the employee is useless. If the worker conscientiously goes about these tasks and completes them, then the Mediocre Manager will take any glory there is to be had. If, however, they fail to successfully complete any designated tasks they will be blamed and branded a failure. Very few senior managers look behind the task and evaluate it to see if it is truly of worth. In this instance, the Respectful Manager would never give tasks without value to the organisation. Everything is directed by the Respectful Manager to one purpose and that is to create value for the business owners, or in a non-profit environment, for their clients. But the Mediocre Manager will operationalise tasks which are politically expedient. If it means producing *n* number of widgets he will do so; if it is to serve *n* number of clients he will do so. However, the he will not innovate unless it is required by those whom he wishes to impress.

The Mediocre Manager is the star of networking; this gives him future contacts to engage in reciprocal activity to rise higher up the corporate ladder. Thus, they swing from position to position like Tarzan in the corporate jungle in search of success. Therefore it is imperative that the Mediocre Manager has an army of supportive workers to aid this upward movement, while any recalcitrant ones must be weeded out. And it is at this point that the bullying and character assassination begins. They have no conscience about it, they just see it as necessary to do, otherwise it would make the manager concerned look bad. Dissent hinders their own self-promotion.

So that is why bullying starts with a Mediocre Manager. You can say that they are innocents playing in a larger power game dominated by the big-salaried CEOs. That is also the reason why we see so much emphasis given on what the 'big boys' have to say, whereas the reality is that their success depends on stripping assets, denuding staffing levels and passing on more work to the hapless few who are left. Great balance sheets and immediate profit and loss outcomes, but in the long term horrendous for the organisation. Organisations will so often fail or become targets for acquisition or merger as they become weakened within the marketplace.

The other big problem that Malevolent Managers face is when outside forces create a dwindling market and new customers have to be found or production will collapse. This puts them under immense pressure for the co-workers to produce more in less time. This is stressful for the manager and he will definitely take it out on some poor hapless worker. Usually the targets will be minority groups, as any Mediocre Manager knows you do not irritate your potential helpmates, so if he looks around the room, he can pick on those who are of ethnic or gender minority and immediately the bullying starts.

Passing on blame to minorities is seemingly a clever way so that the co-worker cannot answer back in the face of being dismissed. Blaming targets for work that is of poor quality when it is nothing to do with the person is often seen in this situation; not taking the advice of the co-worker is another. Setting up meetings where the co-worker is disparaged and everyone can follow their manager's lead and blame the target for everything that goes wrong is another tactic. I have seen bosses vilifying national, mandatory affirmative action programs in order to embarrass those of the selected minority who are present. It is as if the aggrieved target(s) are not present in the room. Similarly, with promotions, the Mediocre Manager will only select those who will be of use to him, and certainly not any minority worker, unless he is absolutely forced to.

The Respectful Manager, by contrast, will look for diversity in their workforce, as they inherently know that diversity of backgrounds gives additional knowledge that can be applied to the task at hand. Women managers are meant to be more respectful than males, so they will tend to have more women in those positions. This is so unless the woman has learnt the tactics of a Mediocre Manager and is there only by means of her own self-promotion. If this happens, the Respectful Manager will quickly identify the problem and will offer retraining of some sort, for example anger management, leadership courses and so on. The last thing he would want to do is to dismiss that woman because as we know, learned behaviour can be unlearned.

So far we have ascertained that bullying is an art form for Malevolent Managers; now we must look at what is the essence of good management. Many people are innately predisposed to being a Respectful Manager, but others have to study it, so an in-depth look is required.

6   How to identify the Respectful Manager

The Respectful Manager is a good manager. It is easier to pick out what the manager is not, now that we know so much about Malevolent Managers and why. But there still remains a question of who is a good manager. Imagine a black painting with a large solid circle of white paint almost like creating a silhouette, the black background represents who is not, and the circle who is. That is how it was in my doctoral research, co-workers sometimes failed to provide clear information to fill in the circle. They could easily identify what the manager was not, rather than what he was. There is no fuzzy line with the clear circle, it is either black or white. This is exactly how respectful management works. It does not contaminate itself with negative behaviour. It is easy to respond to this by saying black and white is too easy an analogy, surely there are shades of grey? The answer is that there are not. There are no shades of grey. Grey means the manager concerned is inconsistent, and Respectful Managers are totally consistent.

The ideal type of a good manager is the real type

One of the best ways of working out what is good management is to look at the virtues of good behaviour. For many in the Christian world there are three commonly cited virtues: Faith, Hope and Charity, but in other religions there are many more. The ancient Egyptians defined six virtues of Truth, Balance, Order, Law, Morality and Justice. Whereas modern day Buddhism has: Right View, Right Mindfulness and Right Concentration, which leads to Loving Kindness to All, Compassion, Altruistic Joy, and Equanimity (which is learning to accept praise and blame). Although I would like to say I lead a good life, I and others need more guidance than this.

Basically, the virtues describe what is ideal human behaviour. We all accept that we do not wish to be murdered or have our neighbours steal from us, or for others to treat us badly. We as humans have consensus on the overall idea of virtuousness, that is being good, but pinning it down is rather problematic in the fast-paced world of the workplace.

There are so many takes on what is a virtue and what is not. I use 'The Virtues Project', (1988) which lists more than fifty virtues drawn from all cultures and sacred texts (Virtues Project International Association, 1991). This project is available to all and covers all positive human behaviour. Some examples may appear repetitive or mere elaborations, others we may consider not applicable to the workplace, so I have chosen from the long list of virtues and used it with a model that I devised some years back for determining what constitutes emotional energy. Positive emotional energy is used by Respectful Managers, and negative emotional energy is used by the other four malevolent types. Remember the theme of consistency, if a person is positive in one virtue and is lacking another, then the person concerned is malevolent and therefore using negative energy.

I estimate that there are three dimensions to our life force energy, and each dimension has a negative extreme and a positive extreme. These dimensions are Connection, Appreciation and Trust (known as the CAT model$^{©}$). The three positive emotions these dimensions create are Love, Joy and Confidence respectively, the three negative emotions, respectively again, are Anger, Sadness and Fear. To sum up:

1   Connection gives Anger at one end and Love at the other;
2   Appreciation generates Sadness at the negative end and Joy at the other; and finally,
3   Fear is at the negative end of Trust and Confidence is the opposite.

As we cannot in this day and age express our love for others in the workplace we use the term Respect to explain what we mean.

I analyse behaviour to measure Respectful Managers on these three criteria as the basis of my work. Therefore, the Respectful Manager would respect others, appreciate others' work joyfully, and have confidence in herself and her co-workers. A Malevolent Manager would be showing signs of anger, sadness often

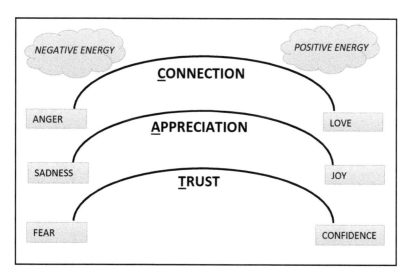

Figure 6.1 The CAT© model

disclosed through envy and greed (remember their drive for power and control) and fear, as they cannot trust others to give them what they want.

Therefore, grouping the virtues that are applicable from the Virtues Project we develop a classification as in Table 6.1, which shows the foundation of key performance indicators grounded on virtues and according to the positive energy of our life force.

Respectfulness

From the three positive values of Love, Joy and Confidence we can develop key performance indicators that are the most important for any organisation of their management, but ignored by many.

Table 6.1 The virtues and KPIs shown by the positive emotion of respect

Positive energy value	Virtue	Performance indicator
	Acceptance	Being compassionate to everyone
	Caring	
	Charity	
	Compassion	
	Courtesy	Being kind and caring to others
	Devotion	
	Dignity	
Connection dimension	Empathy	
	Fairness	Being fair to all
	Faithfulness/loyalty	
	Forebearance	
	Forgiveness	
Respect	Gentleness	Being committed to working with others
	Helpfulness	
	Humility	
	Kindness	
	Mercy	Being focused on what is good
	Openness	
	Self-discipline	
	Sincerity	
	Tact	Having high self-esteem

Being compassionate

Compassion is a major feature of a Respectful Manager; they have a genuine compassion for their co-workers and families. Therefore, they do not insist on long work hours, or frequent drinks after work or at lunchtime. Compassion is the origin of caring and looking after people. They are able to put themselves into another's shoes and understand how they feel. Often this is where good working conditions come from, even the installation of employee assistance programs, crèches and leave allowances. I often counsel managers, when they realise that they are angry with someone, that if they use compassion they will understand that person much better and the anger will ease and turn into mild respect at least. It is the first step in knowing that you have that painted white circle.

A Respectful manager will also show courtesy and consideration of others. This is not about door opening, but being polite, not swearing or using foul language. When I hear bad language in a workplace I am appalled, as it is a primary sign of disrespect. Being courteous includes respecting elders, everyone being treated the same with no favourites. They ensure that customers and co-workers are best served. This desire stems from compassion, so if you are not quite sure whether your manager is Respectful or not, then check out how courteous and considerate he or she is to others.

Forgiveness is in my mind part of the virtue of compassion, as true compassion always forgives, no matter what has happened, or how horrific the offence may be. Many people confuse forgiveness with allowing the perpetrator to get away with their behaviour and therefore to avoid the consequences. This is not so. Real forgiveness never condones the behaviour in question. Rules, including the rule of law, must be observed. We cannot allow ourselves to ignore misbehaviour.

Consider some wrongdoing that has happened in the workplace whereby a co-worker is hurt, physically or emotionally. When it comes out about the misconduct, the target can feel righteous in demanding an apology, and that is a good step to take. But there is one more step to take and that is on the receipt of the apology, the target then undertakes the process of forgiveness. After the injured party has undertaken true forgiveness, if the two parties bump into each other, each can be civil to the other. The perpetrator has learnt an important lesson in life, and the target has put boundaries in place so that it will not happen again. A perfect solution has been found in this situation.

However, what about the situation of: 'I will forgive but I will never forget.' This halfway state of mind is only fooling the wronged individual. Forgiveness allows people to move on in their lives, to not be locked in with the anger and hate of the misdemeanour. One can never really forget, but what the person is in fact stating is 'I will not move on from the hurt.' It is possible to achieve, through true forgiveness, a sense of calm and well-being despite the most awful travesties that can overcome you. Organisations are not terribly good at forgiving and many people leave due to unresolved matters. A Respectful Manager will do whatever he can to resolve a negative situation. This is where mercy comes in with forgiveness and is at the heart of the act of forgiving. Being merciful is still being just, but it is ensuring that punishment for the misdeed is fitting and not an over- or under-reaction. I found in my managerial fraud study that many employers gave good references to their fraudster managers just in order to get rid of them. Of course, the sensible option is to call in the police, but it does not happen in all cases, and so the fraudster manager slips into the next organisation to defraud. This, therefore, was not an act of mercy, rather an act of fear to get rid of someone quickly.

Being kind and caring

The positive energy of the connection dimension is called love, or in the workplace we call it respect. This is defined in the Virtues Project as having many of the virtues that are connected with being kind and caring. Acceptance of all co-workers and others in the organisation reigns. Remember the rude jokes, the office gossip? Respectful managers do not participate in this. They certainly do not repeat such things, as they basically accept others for what they have to offer. This is good news for human resource managers, as a person with disabilities for instance, receives a hearing rather than a flat 'No!' A Respectful Manager will always try to find a way to integrate such a person into the workplace, because they see the value in the individual, not the disability. If there is value, then a placement would be easy with appropriate due diligence to the person's work area and flow of work.

Along with being friendly, the Respectful Manager is helpful. A Mediocre Manager may use this as a tactic to get co-workers onside, but a Respectful Manager actually means to help. This can be in all manner of ways, inside and outside the workplace; helping others is an indication of generosity. Respectful Managers give their time and resources where appropriate. They help because of their nature, not because they want you to vote for them in the next round of promotions. There is no expectation of reciprocity, it is a selfless act of kindness. One of the amazing things that co-workers see is that their Respectful Manager will help them in their careers, so that they are given training and or development to further themselves. If it is appropriate for someone to be acting in a position that is above their own, the Respectful Manager will assist probably with mentoring and guidance, which will always be kindly given.

An unusual virtue to consider for a Respectful Manager is devotion. This is not in a religious or obsessive sense regarding the organisation, but it is an upholding of the work at hand, not being diverted with extraneous matters like networking and being absent from the workplace. Most Respectful Managers will work the extra hours to complete a task, but you will also see them clocking off work when most people leave as well. They then devote their time to their families and friends and those who need their help in the community.

Two virtues that seem to hang together are friendliness and gentleness. Being friendly is part of the Respectful Manager's repertoire, they are genuine in their feelings, they like people, otherwise they would not be managers. Gentleness means that there is no need for people to be impolite and abrupt. There is every need in fact, to take time to listen to co-workers and evaluate how they are doing. Respectful Managers always are courteous, polite and friendly within the time constraints of their work. This leads to workplaces flowing with good humour, generosity to each other and politeness too. If you have a workplace that is like that, then stay, as you have a Respectful Manager on your hands and they are in short supply in this world.

Caring is very natural to a Respectful Manager. They care, very much, about their colleagues. Most often to the point of worrying about individuals that need extra looking after. They will show this in their actions about the organisation and co-workers. A Mediocre Manager will say the words, but Respectful Managers will demonstrate through their actions. This may come about through occupational health and safety improvements, fair work and pay conditions and so on. Look for who implements these things then it will point to a Respectful Manager at the source.

Sincerity and tact go together because if an individual is truly sincere, tact will be employed more often than not. The reason being is that to be sincere is to be able to impart the truth to another in an authentic way. Tact is kindness so that the recipient is not upset by the necessary commentary but encouraged and given the opportunity to change.

Being fair

Empathy is a natural part of respect and is basically being able to be with a person, without judgement and without being sucked in to a person's story. Just being there, is a wonderful element of compassion, as the person on the receiving end will be grateful. Being fair is a virtue that many managers forget about in the daily performance of their work. Being hasty in judgements does not leave a lot of room for fairness. It is far better, and this is what a Respectful Manager does, to step back and ask the question, is the matter at hand fair to all? If that is the case, then the decision can go ahead, but if not, it cannot and will not be made.

Committed to working with others

Respectful Managers insist on clean back offices, toilets, reception and work areas. When you are next in a hotel, take a look down a 'Staff only' exit and you will be able to see if the hotel treats its employees well. Walls will be painted, clear signage, floors clean, free from clutter. This is very impressive, and I try to take a peek wherever I am staying. This goes for any back office as well. A Respectful Manager will not want his staff working in dirty conditions, which is why cleanliness is a virtue in the workplace.

Faithfulness and loyalty are a distinct characteristic of the Respectful Manager; they will always stand by their co-workers and their organisation. They are not the ones to jump ship at any sign of trouble. If the media catches one to make a statement about a particular situation, a Respectful Manager will always say the best that he or she can. This will not lead to dishonesty, it is believing in an organisation and wanting it to survive whatever has hit it, and Respectful Managers have a much higher rate of survival than those controlled by mediocre or tyrant management, as it stands to reason that Respectful Managers having nothing else but the organisation to focus on, so they will achieve it, whereas the Malevolent Managers whose only goals are to better themselves to increase their power and control, will surely fail.

Being focussed on what is good

Self-discipline is at the core of consistency. Things like behaviour, virtues shown, moral codes, are all consistent. There will be times when it would be easy for the Respectful Manager to take short cuts, or even add waffle or embellishments to pad out speeches or written communications. But this sort of activity would not be undertaken as this is the sphere of Malevolent Managers, not of those who respect others.

Choosing the right path can be difficult but beneficial for the organisation, and is all part of self-discipline, rather than the punctuality or tidy desks that we tend to associate with this virtue. It reaches far beyond that. Self-discipline is the basis for adherence to one's moral code, and not being waylaid by other temptations. In the workplace there are many inducements for a manager. Defrauding a company may be very easy for someone with power, but Respectful Managers desist through self-discipline. Using power for other purposes than that of stewardship, like self-aggrandisement or self-promotion, is not in their repertoire.

Not many people know of the virtue of forbearance, as it is a virtue requiring self-control and patience. Many Asian families practice this behaviour by taking the long view of goals to be achieved several generations down the line. In our fast-paced world everything is instantly available and encouraged to be so by massive advertising and financed by those who make a living out of lending money at high rates. Similarly, Respectful Managers will not be spending their budgets on gadgets and the latest device until it is proved to be a good addition to the organisation. They will take the long view, probably much to the annoyance of many an IT manager, and carry over budgets at the year's end in order to apply the benefits of such caring to many of their co-workers as possible.

Forbearance would be seen as part of self-discipline by many, and that thinking would not go astray. Seeing a manager exert self discipline is truly wonderful instead of seeing the dreadful 'firing from the hip' type of management. Many politicians tell us that they are in control, but more often than not their behaviour leads us to conclude that their decisions are very much ad hoc processes. Their policies are never formulated for the long run, neither are they self-disciplined enough to keep their own fingers out of other people's budgets. The reader may suspect that I hold little regard for politicians and the like, but it is only the absence of Respectful Management that I deplore.

High self-esteem

Respectful Managers not only have kindness for others but they are kind to themselves, which results in high self-esteem. This includes forgiveness and learning from mistakes for the individual concerned. This means that they are not conceited, neither are they self-promoting to gain positions that they are unable to cope with. Malevolent Managers have at their core low self-esteem, despite shows of the opposite. A narcissist is one who needs constant attention, as without it they fear that there may be nothing inside. For a Respectful Manager, there is no false sense of self-worth. If they draw attention to themselves it is for a good reason for all to see.

Another virtue that seems at odds with present day life is dignity. If a manager is dignified it does not mean airs and graces and tilting a pinky finger out while having a cup of tea. It means that a Respectful Manager has a natural air about her that co-workers look up to. Slipping on a banana peel may create an uproar at work as co-workers stifle laughs. A dignified person will laugh alongside the workers. Using self-awareness to say appropriate things about the incident so that others will join in with. Being angry to whomever left the banana skin on the floor is not dignified. Losing one's temper is another undignified act. It is important that a manager is able to keep self-control, and this can only happen with high self-esteem. If the manager is hurt and cries out loud, this is not loss of control. It is a sign that he has hurt himself and first aid or even an ambulance is required. There are many situations where we can lose our dignity; it is important to step up to help such a person, just as we would like to be helped in our own loss of dignity moments, particularly when we grow old or infirm.

Humility is a virtue that the Respectful Manager will display. They do not boast about their achievements, their certificates may be up on the wall, but they are not given to talking about them or one-upping others, apart from in friendly banter that is. This is quite a distinctive trait, as Tyrant and Mediocre Managers will self-promote with every chance they get. If you are in the position of senior management, you will find that you will be bombarded with self-promoting activities from the lower ranks. This is quite a problem, as it must be understood that a Respectful Manager will not do that. Of course, at promotion time, he may talk about achievements, but it will always be in relation to his co-workers. Some are so enthusiastic that one feels that the co-worker is being put up for promotion, rather than the Respectful Manager in question. Grabbing the limelight for recognition of good works done in the workplace is the home of Malevolent Managers and the truth is often that some poor co-worker has been slaving away on the project, only to have all the glory taken away from him, thanks to a merciless Malevolent Manager. True humility allows the real actor to come forth and show to the audience the authenticity within. Giving credit for work where it is due is the mark of the Respectful Manager, whereas a Mediocre Manager will claim personal credit believing that this will make him look better.

Openness is another mark of only the Respectful Manager. It is as if they have a window to their soul. Watching a Respectful Manager at work is a joy, as you can see the very heart of what is truly happening. With Malevolent Managers, there is deceit, fraud and lies, all in place to ensure that you do not see the real person inside. It makes you wonder why they would not act in a transparent way, but they want to keep secret their aspirations as they know that these would not be tolerated by their co-workers. If you opened up a Malevolent Manager you would see all sorts of hidden frailties and 'sins' that they feel they must cover up. In fact, they are as frail as we all are and there is no need to be afraid. Some want to hide their background from others, others want to hide their vices underneath their own virtues, which of course is impossible to achieve.

Appreciation

The dimension of Appreciation covers many virtues from sacrifice to awe, from service to understanding, and KPIs have been developed accordingly.

Awe

Being able to demonstrate the virtues of awe and wonderment is again in the Respectful Manager's repertoire, but coming from appreciation of the environment, fellow human beings and their products or services, the organisations that they manage themselves and with each organisation there is an originator of one person or a group. We forget to be in wonder in our modern world but if we sit back for a minute we can see beauty in everything, no matter how ugly it may seem.

Awe can take us to be grateful the smallest kindness, the act of service that is often overlooked. The Americans will often say 'Have a nice day', the equivalent of the French phrase *bon journée*, but how many reply with a 'thank you'? Not many, and when it is done the speaker is a bit surprised at the acknowledgement. A Respectful Manager will take time to say that he is in awe of what the individual does, or how he does it and so on. This is embodied in the theory of Quality Assurance, that there is appreciation of the smallest acts of quality.

Mindfulness is an interesting virtue; one of the early exponents of mindfulness was the Catholic nun, Saint Teresa of Lisieux. She would put her heart and soul into the little things, from scrubbing a floor to polishing candlesticks.

Table 6.2 The virtues and KPIs shown by the positive emotion of joy

Positive energy value	Virtue	Performance indicator
	Awe/wonder	
	Cheerfulness	Appreciating the workplace
	Creativity	
	Discernment	
	Enthusiasm	
	Excellence	
Appreciation dimension	Generosity	Being a cheerful optimist
	Gratitude	
Joy	Hope/optimism	
	Idealism	
	Joyfulness	
	Mindfulness	Being creative
	Resilience	
	Sacrifice	
	Steadfastness	
	Thankfulness	
	Tolerance	Being discerning of what is good
	Understanding	

Mindfulness is about putting all your energy into the detail of the here and now. Another word for it is concentration. Many of us know how it feels when our mind is totally absorbed with reading a book, for instance. Despite what is going on around us, a book that is engrossing makes us feel a part of it. The mind is transported to the task at hand, reading.

Mindfulness is the latest trend today to instil peace into busy minds that are in overdrive. This turmoil in our minds is at best low grade anxiety, and for most people it is from high levels of stress. In reality mindfulness is like an awakened meditation; being mindful is self absorbing, transporting us into our very being. Using mindfulness the Respectful Manager is able to concentrate on managing rather than being diverted by distractions, to assist and look after his co-workers to the maximum. He operates his stewardship carefully, not caring about his ambitions and does not waste his time on plots and schemes that will advance him up the ladder. That is left to the Malevolent Managers who are only mindful of their careers.

Thankfulness is an expression of the emotion of joy. We are truly thankful when we see bad things go away and become the past. After each world war, people were truly thankful that the evil of war had finished. But what happened in each post-war experience was that Malevolent Managers saw opportunities to take advantage of to the detriment of others. A Respectful Manager will be thankful and not do this sort of self-aggrandisement. If a service has been done, no matter how little, the Respectful Manager will always give his thanks. A Mediocre Manager may copy this behaviour, but it will be noticed that thanks are only given to certain people, or on certain occasions. Their inconsistency is noticeable, and this type of behaviour is not part of the suite of behaviours that a Respectful Manager has. When I am in the board room and I hear people say thank you to the person who brings refreshments, I am pleased. However, if they don't say thank you for attending, but other things, you know you have a Malevolent Manager on your hands as it is inconsistent behaviour showing itself again. Subtle clues, but a Respectful Manager will always say thank you when it is due.

Being cheerful

From awe comes cheerfulness. If you think about the opposite of what that is, sadness comes from a lack of awe and wonderment, the individual is without such joy. However, it can be obtained through the route of appreciation, and that is to appreciate how well off one is. To remain cheerful in desperate times is a virtue related to optimism. I have developed a reputation in my family that I am the eternal optimist. They have seen me struggle through very bad times, and once the blow of the next calamity that hits me is appraised I then point out that there are other ways to get by, and so on. This keeps a person cheerful, and also more healthy as there is less time spent on falling into anxiety and depression. I still have days of being depressed, so I cannot do this 100 per cent of the time, but most times I can. My future always looks bright to me, no matter what my circumstances. Respectful Managers know how to cheer up others as well, and they lift up their co-workers with their cheerfulness and optimism.

I have met many enthusiastic managers, and it is interesting that most of them are indeed of the Respectful type. Enthusiasm comes from the depths of our souls. Along with cheerfulness, enthusiasm allows even the most boring of work to be undertaken, as it is seen as necessary to achieve the objective at hand. Enthusiasm is the energy of any task, and managing people is the major task of a manager. Therefore, it has to be done in a directed manner, to no matter what the work is at hand, be it carving a new road in the desert or making lace curtains, enthusiasm oils the machine of work.

Gratitude is what every single one of us needs to feel good in this life. It is a sense of worthwhileness that bestows upon the person the feeling of being included. Respectful Managers do say thank you to those who have given a service. They recognise the time and effort of the person who delivers the action, and give their thanks accordingly. Again, it is appreciation at the bottom of this virtue, and if you have gratitude bestowed on others around you by a manager, you can be fairly sure that this manager is of the Respectful type.

The twin virtues of tolerance and understanding are based in appreciation of others. Respectful Managers will tolerate individuals as they know who they are and why they act as they do. It is a reflection of Joy; as we bring different talents and gifts to the workplace, they appreciate what we bring. A feature of this is having a diversified workplace, where discrimination is not allowed. You will see people with disabilities, women in executive roles, not purely supervisory, co-workers with different backgrounds and heritage. The virtue of tolerance is not however, acceptance of bad behaviour. The Respectful Manager has rules in place that are there for a reason. While the manager will maybe understand why the person is disobeying the rules, the manager will not accept that type of performance from his co-workers. Tolerance is about understanding others to the point that they are willing to have them join the team as they know what that person can offer.

Joyfulness is the basis for the positive energy of appreciation. I have covered this earlier, but recognise the Respectful Manager's art of joyfulness does not mean cracking jokes every tea-time, or wearing a smile to cover up the sadness underneath, like a clown. A wonderful example of joyfulness comes to mind when I was working in a large organisation, and a reply I would get from an employee that wasn't in my division to my How are you? question, was always a joyful reply: 'Absolutely stupendous!' I almost wanted to go out of my way to ask him the same question to get that amazing reply. It made me smile, it spread joy in the workplace. Amazing, as it was only two words. He was a beacon shining in the gloomy darkness of a mediocre-managed section, no-one cared to work there, but he did, as it was another day that brought joy for him and those around him.

I have combined hope with optimism, as these two virtues lean on each other. Where cheerfulness lies, also lies hope. When you take away someone's hope, then that is the road to depression and possibly suicide. Viktor Frankl was a prisoner in a German concentration camp and found that those who survived all had a wife at home, perhaps children, or returned to run an important business. It was these subjects that allowed the survivors to occupy their minds, and that hope was there in their daily thoughts. As he was a psychiatrist previously and involved with treating female suicidal patients it was only natural for him to make this observation (2008).

And of course, there is all the great work done by Martin Seligman (1998) who, as I quote below, worked out that the world is made up of two sorts of people:

> The defining characteristic of pessimists is that they tend to believe bad events will last a long time, will undermine everything they do, and are their own fault. The optimists, who are confronted with the same hard knocks of this world, think about misfortune in the opposite way. They tend to believe defeat is just a temporary setback, that its causes are confined to this one case. The optimists believe defeat is not their fault: Circumstances, bad luck, or other people brought it about. Such people are unfazed by defeat. Confronted by a bad situation, they perceive it as a challenge and try harder.

The Respectful Manager cannot be a pessimist. That would run contrary to the virtues which form part of his character. Even the most die-hard pessimist can learn optimism. It has been noted in numerous studies that optimistic people have more happiness in their lives, make more sense of what life is all about, and that they contribute to a healthy world.

Optimism allows the manager to bring positive energy into the workplace, so that co-workers can be re-energised and focus on goals, despite setbacks and hardships. There were a couple of stories told by co-workers in my research that reflected the optimism of their Respectful Manager. One such account was when the firm lost their most important customer. Such is the danger of small businesses, that often their customer base is difficult to expand. And when it was final, rather than fire everyone and give up, the manager concerned built up a new organisation focussed on giving similar services to a different customer base. This is the sort of positive energy of optimism that flows to others naturally and freely when faced with obstacles.

Resilience is in managerial terms being able to bounce back after setbacks in the organisation. It is not only linked with optimism, if you like, it is the actual performance of optimism. Malevolent Managers use their resilience to avenge themselves on those who created the setback. They will never forget the difficulty which has befallen them and will mastermind schemes of revenge. This is not resilience, this is pure revenge. And that is never on the radar of the Respectful Manager. The less downtime a manager has, the quicker he can get back on to his feet to get back to the job. Resilience is also passed on to his co-workers who see this and how quickly he is able to return to work, so that it sets a role model to all, and the organisation quickly gets back to what it is meant to be doing. Disaster planning is all about operationalising resilience. You don't have such a plan in your workplace? Well then, it means that you have malevolent management in your workplace, and they do not care for you or your colleagues one iota. A Respectful Manager will always have a disaster plan. It may not be written down, but he will have it in his mind should disaster befall the workplace. Whenever I hear of workplaces with lousy risk management in place, I know that we have to find a Respectful Manager in the organisation to rectify it immediately. Quite a few organisations which have suffered large scale commercial disasters have not had simple measures in place which could have averted the problem. Natural disasters happen, and once-in-a-lifetime events always catch out Malevolent Managers.

Creative

Surprisingly perhaps, to many, creativity comes out of the appreciation dimension. We cannot be creative if we are constrained in our environment. A worker who is stuck on the factory floor repeating the same menial tasks, cannot be creative. If we appreciate our environment and take the opportunity that is open to us, we can apply our creativity in our lives. Many people say that meetings are a waste of time. What they should be doing in those meetings is to discuss new ways of doing things in order to take less time, or be more profitable, or easier for colleagues. The dull lifeless meeting is a chore to attend precisely because it does not allow creativity or problem solving. It takes up the valuable time of those who could be better employed innovating or implementing creative strategies. A mark of a good manager is to throw open the meeting for ideas. If this is done often, attendees will become used to working in an environment that allows ideas, no matter how whacky they may sound, and even the most introverted will feel empowered to contribute creatively.

The next virtue that a Respectful Manager will exhibit is linked with optimism, and that is idealism. This may not necessarily be 'blue sky' stuff; it can actually be well grounded in solid research on a bed of evidence. What it means is that we can spread the good news of our forecasts. Most business plans are like this. The difference is that the Respectful Manager will make a judgement and share it with his or her co-workers. Sharing the future with others is a way of defining what is right in the organisation and showing how others can make their contribution. Such is idealism for a Respectful Manager. They give hope, prove the nay-sayers wrong, and make happier lives for their co-workers in the process.

From the depths of appreciation comes the pursuit of excellence. We have seen it in our machines, our cars, planes, computers, software, everywhere we look, it is the drive for excellence that has created all that is positive in our world. Poor design or workmanship has resulted in accidents and even deaths.

There is one car manufacturer that stands alone in the industry. Rolls-Royce are known worldwide for their cars that are hand made all the way through their manufacture. Now car makers can achieve even better tolerances in their new designs that outdo the charm of being hand made. Apparently, it is only the paintwork that is automated to give a better consistency than that can be achieved by hand. The pursuit of excellence has made the firm as renowned as it is, due to this one virtue extolled by their founders. Price never mattered, it was always about taking pride in being the best.

Excellence can be in any form in product or service delivery, if you try to do your very best, then you should be rewarded by being appreciated. Respectful Managers automatically look for excellence in their work and show their appreciation accordingly. This gives the co-worker reassurance that their work matters, and that it is appreciated by management. Far too often work is overlooked and there is little feedback about a person's performance in this regard. Even if you are cleaning a toilet, your work of excellence should be noted, not just by yourself but by others too. I often stop to say that I appreciate how a toilet is particularly clean in public places if the attendant is present. No one else bothers but these cleaners are keeping communicable disease at bay through their mostly unappreciated work.

Sacrifice is also part of the appreciation set of virtues that a Respectful Manager upholds. For himself, he will judge a situation, and when it demands it he will make sacrifices for long term gain. This is based in his optimism, knowing that in the long term, things will work out. He would not make his co-workers sacrifice anything if he was not doing it himself. Bonuses that are handed out to the senior executive team when times are hard are the signs of Malevolent Managers at work. The opposite of joy is envy and greed, so watch out for these tell-tale signs in your workplace. The Respectful Manager will not be a part of such borderline criminal activity. He would hand back the bonus to the board and not partake in such greed. That is truly respectful management, to take what is honestly theirs, not at the behest and example of others.

Discerning

Discernment is another virtue that the Respectful Manager possesses. Having already made the connection with others, discernment is required in order to determine who can be trusted, in order to progress to the next dimension of Trust. It is about appreciating a person's gifts and abilities. Over the last 50 years, the Myers-Briggs Type Indicator (1995) offers a typing of sixteen categories of people with their varying gifts. It is logical to assume that one person can be good at one thing, and another person with another. Myers-Briggs blew the doors wide open on how to utilise people at their best in an organisation. To recognise that they have varying talents in the workplace is the first step of discernment. This sort of people-judging is what a Respectful Manager does best. All the co-workers in my research reported that their Respectful Manager trained and developed them accordingly. This presents a golden opportunity to the co-workers to achieve their career objectives within the framework of the organisation. They may even leave if they have out-grown their organisation, but it will be after a number of years while he or she receives the considered and fair training that is required, as judged by the Respectful Manager.

Discernment is not being swayed by the crowd. Just because 99 per cent of the people think that something is the best way to go, the 1 per cent can still easily discern the right way to progress. That is why most organisations that are run by Respectful Managers are profitable, as they make use of all their resources. They are unstoppable in this, as it is their duty to discern correctly. Obviously, this can make the manager unpopular, but in the end the judgement call is correct as they have taken the time and effort to find the right answer.

Respectful Managers show their acts of service by attending to their employees. They are renowned for developing their people. Every co-worker in my study mentioned this attribute. This is one of the reasons why staff stay, as their manager looks after them now and helps them to prepare for the future. People are sent on appropriate training courses. Perhaps a detailed development plan is put together for the employee and the first steps are put in place within the allowance of the budget. We know that we are all not the same, and that we have different talents, Respectful managers pick up on that and develop their people accordingly.

Steadfastness and certitude are often in short supply at planning meetings as managers chop and change their priorities to what suits them best. Of course, the environment can change rapidly and everyone must adapt, but I have often witnessed managers grabbing portfolios if they perceive them as advantageous. A Respectful Manager will not do that but he will also protect his co-workers. They appreciate this virtue in their manager as then they can rely on him and form views of the future that are steady, reliable and reachable. Anxiety eats away any chance of surviving change; steadfastness is the lighthouse on the rocky shore which guides people to safety. Without steadfastness, we live in an environment of turbulence, not knowing what is what from day to day and there lies madness.

Trust

Now we turn to the last dimension of Trust. At the one end is Fear with negative energy, and the other end of positive energy sits Confidence.

Being confident to be accountable and committed

A Respectful Manager will want to have accountability with responsibility for his portfolio. He will take steps with consideration and thought to provide what is best for his team. This means that he is also willing to delegate and offer other co-workers accountability in their own areas. However, that is only done on the proviso that "the buck stops here" at his desk. Look at who is being blamed for any error, and then look back at who is making the accusation, then you have pinpointed a Malevolent Manager. Blame is a tool used by Malevolent Managers who are so insecure that they cannot stand up and take the punishment for the misdemeanour, and are feckless in what they are committed to.

Commitment is a natural virtue for Respectful Managers; they may have ambition, but for the sake of others will stay until the job is done. This means that these managers are reliable. They want to see the outcomes of their goals happen and development of their staff. This gives the certainty in a wild environment that enterprises can face with upsurging technologies and methodologies.

Respectful Managers also show courage. They will stand up for their teams, defend their co-workers and budgets to anyone else, and are courageous enough to try new work routines to replace ineffective old ones. Courage comes in many forms and is frequently not recognised at the top, where innovation is not looked upon kindly as it may be believed to destabilise the organisation. Most managers will try to find a senior manager who they can persuade the virtues of the new ideas, but boards should allow any manager to give a short presentation on what would improve work flows and so on.

Table 6.3 The virtues and KPIs shown by the positive emotion of confidence

Positive energy value	Virtue	Performance indicator
	Accountability	
	Certitude	
Appreciation dimension	Confidence	Being confident enough to be fully accountable and committed
	Cooperation	
	Courage	
	Decisiveness	
	Detachment	
	Determination/ perseverance	
	Purposefulness	Being free to be independent in thought and action
	Diligence	
	Endurance	
	Flexibility	
	Fortitude	
Confidence	Honesty/truthfulness	
	Integrity	Being serene in crises
	Moderation	
	Peacefulness	
	Reliability	
	Serenity	
	Simplicity	
	Strength	
	Trustworthiness	Being reliable
	Wisdom	
	Accountability	

Being free to be independent in thought and action

Once positive energy flows through an individual, a serenity ensues which frees them from all sorts of constraints. This means that Respectful Managers will happily co-operate with others, including those outside their teams, even those managers with bad reputations if it helps the company. Often new ways of working can come about from the sharing of ideas at conferences and forums. This is not networking their way up, it is about sharing useful ideas and information that assists everyone.

Another freedom that trust gives is being able to take action through the virtue of decisiveness. It is a prerequisite to be able to make good choices that lead to good decision-making. The other part of decisiveness is to stick with the decision. This gives co-workers once again reliability and confidence in their management. Once a decision is made it will not be undone on a political whim.

Freedom brings flexibility, another virtue of the Respectful Manager. Having the flexibility to accommodate important changes is a necessary attribute of their character. Do not confuse this with chopping and changing with the wind in order to gain advancement. Look to see what is gained by this flexibility and always you will find that it is the good of the organisation that is at heart of the Respectful Manager.

Being able to be detached gives the Respectful Managers the ability to make an unpopular decision. Life is not easier being a Respectful Manager, but it does allow the manager to sleep at night despite the reactions of others. This will only occur when the right decision has been made. The courage behind this is not to be criticised as unpopular as the decision is, it is for the common good of the co-workers.

Being able to achieve goals

There is a small group of virtues that mark the Respectful Manager, and they are having the confidence to persevere, to be determined and purposeful, and to have endurance and fortitude in their lives. This is derived from the basic courage and strength of character underneath that pushes critics aside and helps to persevere against adversity.

Contrary to the other types, Respectful Managers will be diligent in everything that they do. From decision making to planning, to supervising, to ensuring any occupational hazards are dealt with. The whole gamut of managing will be done without harm to others, and without any thoughts of career enhancement. Their relationships with co-workers will be harmonious. Diligence does not mean overworking or being a workaholic. It is doing a job that needs to be done and doing it to the best of your ability. Once it is finished, it is on to the next task. Diligence is not found at the expense of family or close friends by working long hours. The Respectful Manager knows that and always allow time for their family and hobbies. Working smarter, not harder, is the dictum of the Respectful Manager.

Another characteristic of being independent of thought is being honest and truthful. Sadly, this is often lost in organisations where internal politics are being played out. Most people are fed up with this type of internecine warfare. Especially when good employees are needlessly fired or demoted. A Respectful Manager is not drawn into these wars, and when asked to take sides as they often are, they will be truthful to the plaintiff. Honesty is also required in performance evaluations. There are many ways to discuss under-performance. It is not necessary to hurt the individual concerned. Appraising requires insight into what the person is able to do well, as well as what he is unable to do. So often the evaluation is the start of redeployment elsewhere, or retraining if the person concerned is unsuitable in their current role.

Also, the same process will happen when the manager is faced with someone who is untrainable through a variety of reasons usually down to laziness, poor work ethic, and lack of moral compass. The Respectful Manager will always use truth and show the individual concrete examples of their untrainability. The examples should be written evidence that could stand in a court of law. It is highly unusual for us to be untrainable, but there will always be someone out there who is. Psychopaths entering organisations, for example, can easily fall into this category and some people with certain personality disorders. I am not being judgemental here, it is a fact of life that these people exist and once that decision is made, then the Respectful Manager will let the person go. As a social worker I have worked with such individuals in the past and understand this type of dis-ability; if the organisation has the resources, I would suggest that shadowing is a good way to turn around a person to be more productive.

Associated with honesty is integrity, and we can guess that the Respectful Managers have this. They are strong characters; Goffman would be proud of them, as they would have the integrity guaranteed by their authenticity. It also is associated with fortitude, as the manager will be under the spotlight for his decisions in a malevolently managed organisation. If a Respectful Manager had been dismissed, I would know instantly that the previous organisation was malevolent. The job then is to find a respectfully managed organisation that will admire these virtues rather than dispute them and hide from them.

On this matter, my prediction is that within 2 years a dismissal will take place. This 24-month period is based on the fact that the Malevolent Managers have a chance to build up their case and make it impossible for the Respectful Manager to stay. When the emotional energy in an organisation is opposed to the manager concerned, it is like two opposing magnets being pushed together. It makes it absolutely impossible for the differing energy person to stay. This accounts for many unemployed managers that I used to see in my daily practice. I would cal-culate how long they had been with their last organisation and amaze people on being correct in every instance. Similarly, and far less often, I would come across a Malevolent Manager dismissed out of a positive energy organisation. And of course, they were only happy to find themselves another malevolent organisation.

Being peaceful

Moderation is a key virtue for the Respectful Manager, it ties in with self-dis-cipline so that they do not get carried away with the latest fads at work. They view things with a measured eye. Moderation is also found alongside simplicity. Things do not have to be complicated. You will find Respectful Managers always simplifying work and work flows in order to assist their co-workers to produce optimally. A manager has to have to have a lot of confidence to go in and moderate other's work, but they have that attribute. And of course, they will do it with respect for those affected. They do not need to ask for extra budget, they work within what is available to achieve optimum work flow, from happy co-workers.

Peacefulness comes from within. There is no fear attached to the Respectful Manager, as he is confident within himself and within his environment. People are attracted to this kind of person as they feel the positive energy that comes out in speech and behaviour. Having a peaceful manager is to many a godsend, as the others surround themselves with busy-ness making a big noise of their work, rather than getting on with it. Their serenity makes them approachable by co-workers, they know that they can pop their head around the door and ask questions. But once the Do Not Disturb sign is up, they respect that, and know that the person will be available soon. Serenity is one of the pleasures of working with a Respectful Manager, as senior managers will know that the most that can be done is being done. Something that Malevolent Managers cannot be trusted to do.

Being reliable

By now you will see that trust is built on the reliability exuded by the Respectful Manager. This leads to trustworthiness. Being reliable is often overlooked in the workplace, and sometimes it is considered that reliability is boring. The better view is that co-workers see the manager as being reliable in their supervision and requests. There are no severe and crushing demands from a Respectful Manager. There are no surprises either.

Punctuality is a linked behaviour; set meal times and going home times are signs of a reliable person. This does not mean to say that they cannot deal with a surprise, of course they can, but they will take their time to deliver their answers and smooth things out. Harmony, the connecting fabric of all these positive virtues, is present and others innately feel it. It is hard for them to describe, but they feel it all the same. Finally, the co-workers realise that their Respectful Manager is trustworthy and has built up a reputation of being wise. Often other co-workers from other teams will spot this virtue and they too will approach the Respectful Manager for advice and wisdom.

Using this approach of looking at virtues is valuable as it gives us the detail that we need for evaluating performance. I found with the co-workers of the non-fraudulent managers that had Respectful Managers that they agreed with such a list. One reason given for the inability of respondents in the study to give more information on why their manager was good is that they have made their decision and put it in the background, while Malevolent Managers have to be watched carefully and so their co-workers' observations are much more elaborate and acute. This may very well be an evolutionary element that we have developed, as keeping a close eye on a deadly sabre-tooth tiger is extremely favourable for survival.

7 Are you a Respectful Manager?

So now we know what to look for with others and also it gives us a foundation to look at ourselves seriously. We know that we are not perfect beings, but we would all like to be considered the next best thing. Unfortunately though, we are all prone to self-delusion.

If you find yourself disagreeing with that last statement and saying 'Not me!' you are all the more likely to be so. The better way of finding out if you are a Respectful Manager is to ask others.

Trusting others

The problem with asking others by doing it yourself via a questionnaire is that you may get biased results from co-workers. For instance, a subordinate who wishes to please you may put in positive answers, and alternatively, an employee who does not like you for whatever reason may put down negative answers. If the questionnaire is handed out by another person, say a human resource manager or consultant, all the better. There has to be complete anonymity for the respondents, so that the co-workers can express their opinions freely. It has to be guaranteed that there will be no reprisals against the respondents and that 'any news is good news'.

If you are in a small organisation and there are not many respondents, then it is time for honest, heart-to-heart conversations. I would also do this with trusted friends. The trust that you need is that they will be honest with you and not wish to appease you to save the friendship. These individuals are few and far between in our lives and they are to be treasured.

Once the information is in, it is time to analyse it. This is not a popular magazine type of inquisition, it is serious-soul searching, and if the co-workers have enough trust in you then you will see what the data have to offer.

There is a way to analyse the data to ensure its veracity, and that is to put into separate piles the answers to the yes/no questions. If you have many answering yes, then that will be an authentic response. Similarly, if the answers are no, then it too can be taken as a truthful response overall. If it is a resounding yes, that you are a Respectful Manager, then to further develop yourself, use the virtues as outlined above, particularly the least developed ones, to provide a well-rounded disposition in your daily routines.

Now what about the other pile of horrible no's to you being a Respectful Manager? This is like gold to you, do not throw it away in a fit of pique. No one likes to hear bad news, especially regarding something so close to your heart as your managerial style. It requires sensitive handling, and I will be producing more work on how to learn and instil the Respectful Executive Impression Management Type, so that everyone can read you more clearly and not confuse you with the malevolent types.

It is very similar to a television reality show that centres on cooking and improving a normal household's diet. There is no bad in this, there is: less good, good, better, best. Many people use fast food to eat in a hurry, yet we know that this is probably not so good as home prepared cooking. The gradual change to eating more nourishing and appropriate portions is to cook at home. Similarly, an Executive Impression Management style can be changed, after all it is an extension of the self, and we know for a fact that people can change dramatically and reject their previous ways of doing things.

Many routines that we incorporate in our daily lives are not truly reflective of us anyway, they are learned behaviours in order to survive and prosper in our world. An ambitious manager does not have to be malevolent, she can still retain her goals, but she can meet them in positive-energy ways. I have ambition, ambition to change the workplaces of the world for the better. Should I give away my Executive Impression Management type of Respectful Management in order to do this? No. In fact, the journey to doing this will be enjoyable and provide lasting change to everyone that I meet, so that they can realise their true potential.

Recently I have seen many old and even ancient works of art. I have been struck how the creators have been able to hone their skills to provide such quality work. I am quite sure that no one said, 'No this cannot be done'. In fact, before the agrarian revolution, a person would not say, 'Today I am going to invent something'. Far from it, they used their skills in their daily work and realised that if you change this widget to that widget you get a result far beyond the imagination. After all, someone invented the wheel.

As early as 6,000 years ago we find evidence that the wheel was invented, before then it was a matter of dragging a load from A to B. The wheel is likely to have been made from disks of tree trunks and branches and certainly potters were using wheels by 5,000 years ago (Kramer, 1963). Once the wheel was invented it meant that discovery of land around Europe was able to occur through plains and forests rather than be located by water. Again, someone somewhere made the intuitive leap to dig out a tree trunk to make a boat, as previously it was reliance on rafts whose reeds were prone to rotting.

We now have the opportunity to make progress more rapidly to help the citizens of the planet. Imagine the joy of producing something new or delivering a service to its best potential. This is why we work, not to make others rich, but to achieve a better way of life for ourselves. And if this includes learning to become a Respectful Manager, so much the better.

How to deal with disjointed feedback

To return to the questionnaire responses, if there is a mixed response, then someone is not being truthful. We know from my research that people really know when they have a Respectful Manager on their hands. They just get stuck for words beyond 'good', 'great', or 'the best'. If you have co-workers who are giving mixed feedback then it is most likely that they are in negative headspace. At this point it is far better to find out why the responses vary, as this aspect points to the respondents rather than the manager in question. It requires sensitivity to handle this; a quiet interview with each respondent may draw out the concerns that people have. Usually it is a projection of their own feelings on to the manager (see a specific example about racism and projection in Reeves, 2000) For instance, an individual whose job it is to plan and evaluate progress may accuse the manager of lacking in planning and claim that the project is going slow because of that. At this point it is important to address the issue of the planner is not able to do the job properly. The next person, who may be responsible for administration of the team, says that there is no trust here, intimating that the manager is untrustworthy. Then the next person says it is all to do with operations that are not being streamlined, and so on. Disjointed feedback, even if all bad, is not necessarily due to the manager in question. Possibly someone is manipulating from the sidelines or there is a power struggle in the team. Helpful resources must be given to resolve the conflict that is going on or the organisation may lose a very good manager.

Setting up performance evaluation

If you are a senior manager or in human resources and want to set up a performance review system, then my advice is to use the points in the questionnaire as the basis for performance. It is not how quickly a person can produce a piece of work, it is how well they do it, without harm but with respect for others. Using the virtues framework gives the qualities that you wish to see in a respectful workplace, as we know that these types of workplaces produce their very best within reasonable times and usually beyond expectations. That is all that is meant to happen. Performance will be at its peak and stay at its peak as co-workers enjoy their work and want to be there every day.

This is not understood by many in the performance management world. The standard key performance indicators derived are usually quantitative rather than qualitative, yet it is quality that determines the job and resulting performance. It is quite simple really. Sure, we can add in some quantitative objectives, like so many widgets or service deliveries a month, but these must be in addition to the virtues that are the foundation of quality management in a workplace. So, use the three-dimensional CAT model of positive energy in your workplace and things will change, some quite rapidly others more slowly, but I can guarantee that it will happen. The virtues are solidly constructed, and they have definite behaviours attached to practising them. Even an obscure one, say forebearance, tells us that we expect tolerance in the workplace, that patience must be had with slower co-workers, that patient encouragement will produce the outputs required. After all, using the opposite of forbearance, impatience, which the world has used in almost every workplace at one time or another, has got people nowhere. So why not try the opposite? Encouragement is enlightenment to the problem at hand.

I have used the Virtues Project's cards in many a meeting. Many are suspicious at first, thinking it is hocus-pocus, black magic or similar. What I do is get all attendees to shuffle the pack and take out a virtue card. These cards have on one side a precise description of the virtue and on the other side the behaviours associated with it. The language is simple, and is used in many a school and community project to raise the level of self-awareness which improves behaviour almost without speaking about it. I then ask each person what their card is, and at this point it is up to the group to give examples of how the person actually does this in real life. It brings out many positive validations in the group, and assists the attendees to produce a really positive performance during the next few hours. You see, people are unaware of the effect of their behaviour on others, and it is a responsibility of a manager to ensure that self-awareness is encouraged.

8   Aspiring to be a Respectful Manager?

Not enough Respectful Managers in the workplace

We need more Respectful Managers in the workplaces around the globe. In studies about ideal type managers there have been estimates that about 15 per cent fall into this category (Bass used a bibliographic technique in 1987). Most people gasp at this statistic, but we know this must be true from our collective experience. There are high rates of bullying in the workplace, and these will be perpetrated by Malevolent Managers of all grades.

It is so prevalent that we can easily convince ourselves that we must be the problem and not them. I had several experiences of malevolent management in one period of my working life and began to think it must be down to me and how on earth was I provoking this response. I was so easily prone to rejection and abandonment from the separation from my mother and being adopted that all I needed was a 'no thank you' and I would be devastated. After my healing process, I began to look at the rejections that I received more objectively and to realise that anyone in my shoes would have felt the same. After a series of bullying incidents, I came to realise that it was, in fact, nothing to do with me. What was happening was the operation of the managerial code of deception and blaming.

During my research when I accidentally came across the Executive Impression Management theory, it was only then that I realised it was down to Malevolent Managers. Because in the literature there is very little said about such poor management. And the last thing that some organisations want is a clever woman manager. This insight led me to re-evaluate my experiences and sadly I realised that at best I had only one manager who I could say was a Respectful type. Regrettably, even after undertaking two migrations, from the UK to Canada and from there to Australia, thereby experiencing three Anglo-Saxon cultures, I can only pinpoint one Respectful Manager.

Drawing back the veil of malevolent management has made me understand the power games that are continuing on a daily basis. Malevolent Managers will actively undermine Respectful Managers, so they usually end up in departments or units that are sheltered from the onslaught of malevolent practices and shield their co-workers accordingly. Far from being valued, they are detested. The only reason that Malevolent Managers put up with the Respectful type is that the latter are able to do something that they cannot do. Maybe this is a particular expertise, or performance of production or service that they are unable to achieve. In which case the Respectful type will be tolerated until they no longer prove useful. Someone who is able to contribute in such a positive manner is protected for the time being. Usually the hidden forces of positive versus negative energy lead to disengagement within 2 years. There will be exceptions to this rule, but they will leave the organisation, or build up a unit geographically removed, or through functionality, or some other delineation. This explains why there are hotspots of brilliant management in large organisations and a lack of uniformity in results. Everyone can point to bad managers, blame circumstances and so on but what they do not realise is that it is the respectfully managed unit which is the anomaly. If they allowed Respectful Managers in, then uniformity would be achieved through repeated successful performance across the board. Yet most organisations' response to hotspots is to rotate Malevolent Managers, or induct new Malevolent Managers into the organisation and produce the same second-rate results. They say that the sign of idiocy is do the same thing twice but expect different outcomes. This means that we have a high level of idiocy in our organisations and recruitment specialists. They are unable to grasp that a Respectful Manager is a specific type, they only see successful performance in results and if the results are poor, then blame someone and get rid of him or her.

What absolutely amazes me is that shareholders and investors do not understand what is going on. As like seeks like, then all you will get is a row of CEOs who try to get the desired monetary performance, without realising that short-term actions produce short term gains, which is equated with success; meanwhile the shell of the organisation that is left from the budget cuts and cutbacks in staff implodes. We are already experiencing the implosion of Britain's National Health Service. This service was the bastion of the new welfare state that was created in Britain after World War II. Before, people had died due to malnutrition, being unable to afford medical services, and many died needlessly young. There was a huge downturn in infant mortality rates with the institution of the welfare state, and a subsequent increase in life expectancy. Most of this is due to the NHS alone. In some areas in Britain, whether or not you will be treated for a life-threatening illness in time depends on where you live. In some income quartiles, most will not be able to afford the full spectrum of medical services, and some in the higher income quartiles will purchase their own through expensive medical insurance and have no need of the NHS. I visualise the service now as a broken spider's web, swinging in the breeze ready to be blown away by a strong gust of wind. Perhaps this will turn around when voters, the true investors of the NHS, say no to further cutbacks and put in a government that respects their wishes. Investors must become aware that they are ultimately responsible for performance of a service, whether good, bad or indifferent.

No glass ceiling: it is a kindergarten fence

This lack of understanding about lack of accountability and responsibility in an organisation leads to aspiring women managers learning malevolent behaviours, which are in turn supported by the resident malevolent management. This will include drinking after hours, having sexual intercourse with those who will help their career, and copying their malevolent behaviours with their co-workers. This happens, and female managers are said to be as bad as males or even worse.

There is not a glass ceiling in place; it is a kindergarten fence. There is an invisible sign that reads 'Join Malevolent Managers or lose out.' Many do not want to do this and prefer to leave. More often the clever ones get bullied out, so that they are no longer a threat to the entrenched macho management style. I have seen one older woman, the senior manager of a large organisation, bewail the fact that she was unable to find other work after she had fulfilled her contract with the organisation. She did not realise that she had left a trail of targets and distraught co-workers behind her, which is testament to the fact she was a Malevolent Manager. And now being doubly crossed, as a woman manager and being older, she was booted out by the system and unable to find work of any consequence. This sad story is rather Faustian in its theme of selling one's soul to the Devil and being damned for the rest of one's life. However, it is highly reflective of what goes on with senior women managers. In a national study that I delivered (Sheridan, 2005) I found that many women managers who were unemployed were bullied out of their jobs by senior managers of either gender.

It is far more effective to not concentrate on affirmative action programmes, although they, together with supportive training, have value and put the emphasis more on generating Respectful Managers irrespective of gender. This is because Respectful Managers will induct more women than will Malevolent Managers. We have university-based business schools but we do not yet have Respectful Management schools, or curricula, or courses. Why is that? This is entirely down to the domination of the elite business education sector by Malevolent Managers. Look up the literature on business ethics and see the struggle that pioneers in this noble area have experienced. We desperately need Respectful Managers, yet no one is trained as such.

Respectful workers become Respectful Managers

Respectful Managers do not suddenly appear on the horizon like the Lone Ranger. At some stage they have been workers themselves and it is from this pool that they arise. So, what would be the characteristics of workers who show Respectful Manager potential? I have developed a list of behaviours that should be evident in any potential candidate.

Characteristics of respectful workers

This person listens attentively to instructions and knows what has to be done accordingly. He or she does a good job with the work at hand. Diligence is the key here, not chasing their way through a job and sitting back for a chat; it is seriously doing the best that is required. If things go wrong they have visibly shown that they can take the criticism appropriately and positively. They may have had the need to check out further, and if you like, are seeking mentoring for their mistakes or errors. I have noticed that they take ownership of mistakes and they really want to take care about their work.

Smiling and being polite is always a good sign. Look for uniformity in expression, any differences are inconsistencies that must *not* be ignored. This belies what is going on underneath the impression management that they are exhibiting. If a person is considered rude, then that is what precisely you will get from this person if appointed: rudeness and impoliteness which fails to connect with others in a positive manner. Remember the song about the crocodile – don't be taken in by his friendly grin. Crocodiles are apparently good smilers, but only at lunch time I suspect. Therefore, look for employees who are socially aware, who take the time to smile and greet people with pleasantries. It is always a good positive energy indicator, as long as it is not lunch time. A hearty 'Hello!' is always a good start to any work situation, and is highly contagious to others.

Similarly, giving feedback to others in an agreeable manner should be noted. It is an important task of the Respectful Manager to be able to do this well. Respectful workers will do this too, but within the limitations of their work role. No temper tantrums are allowed, and if this has been noted then strike that person from the list, as they are simply too emotionally immature to cope with a management position.

You will find that a good worker does not get involved with office politics. They may be forced to listen to it at lunch breaks, but do not need to respond or get caught up in such matters. Discernment is a virtue that should be developed by the individual concerned and the co-worker may be seeing a situation which requires involvement. That is not politics. Political wrangling is all about jockeying for positions of power over others. A Respectful worker would be able to recognise this for what it is. Becoming involved, though, means that the worker has the ability to resolve the situation, and if not then to take the matter to others who have that authority. In Australia we call this dobbing-in, and a worker has to run the gauntlet of being despised by others for their perceived lack of solidarity. Therefore, especially in Australian workplaces it is best to have an independent hotline to which a worker can take such apparent inequities. Obviously this would be very desirable in other countries as well, particularly as the hotline is a most useful tool against managerial fraud (ACFE, 2018).

Sometimes this situation of favouritism is unavoidable, but it has to be faced. The individual in question is made a favourite by another manager or the boss. This system is based on reciprocity and that the favours offered are to be returned later. This can be in any form, including going to bed with someone. Patronage has long been a feature of the workplace, and in the arts has been responsible for the development of outstanding artists. In the normal workplace though, it should not be happening. The favourite has to be polite, but lay boundaries down for the reciprocal demands that this situation will provoke. We sometimes become favourites and are powerless to change the situation, and it may be to the detriment of the budding manager's career. Talking to human resources people should supply options about what to do, and if it does not, the co-worker must request a move to another work role or department. I would even advise a job search if the situation is untenable. This has to be out of hours of course, and carefully done so as not to jeopardise the current work role.

Something that is absolutely required from a co-worker being considered for management, is there is no lying even to cover for others, and especially those little white lies. Someone who tells lies is trying to change the reality of others. This is actually an abusive act, as we all have to work on the basis of truth. If a potential candidate has been known to lie, then a managerial position must be out of the question.

Being sympathetic with other co-workers is another characteristic, showing the underlying connectedness with others that is based on positive energy. Being willing to train others is another good pointer, especially taking the time with their own subordinates to bring them up to speed in their job. The area of customer relations, external and internal, is a useful behaviour to analyse; I would be looking for good relationships with not only customers but with suppliers. Being co-operative is a big indicator of the person's amiability and ability to work together, which of course is needed for the managerial role.

Some people are inordinately untidy; they spill their food, their drink and their work papers everywhere. This is not a good indication of course. I do not mind seeing an untidy desk if and only if at the end of the day the job area or desk is clean and set up for the next day's work. Good timekeeping is also a positive characteristic; this is beyond being punctual for work but also being punctual when leaving the workplace. However, some workplaces demand overtime. This is not necessarily a good thing if it is requested all the time, and certainly if the extra hours are unpaid. It would be expected that a reasonable demand be met with due diligence and care. And another behaviour to be looked for which may seem contrary to diligence, is taking holidays when due. This reflects an internal state of good self-esteem and wanting a work/life balance. After all, there has to be a refreshment of energy outside of work hours and taking vacation time not wanting to accumulate it for later, and without arguing, is a very good indicator.

Finally, an unusual indicator that you are less likely to have a fraudster on your hands, is by observing if they bring their partners or friends to work celebrations. This can be just a picnic in the park or a grand ball but ensure that you know if the person arrives with a partner and stays with that partner in the event, not dumping him in a corner in order to socialise with workmates.

Assessing emotional energy

I can give you a model for assessing your own emotional energy, which is quick and easy to do. Reviewing the dimensions of Connection, Appreciation and Trust in the CAT model referred to earlier, think of putting a 0 per cent against the most negative signs: anger, sadness and fear, and a 100 per cent at the positive ends of the dimensions: respect, joy and confidence, and now think about where you would put yourself on those dimensions today. What I would like you to do is to assess where you are in the dimension of Connection: for instance, is it 50 per cent, or 75 per cent or what? Then do the same again with the other two dimensions. This will give you a total if you add up the scores on each dimension. Now go back to the individual scores; which score was the lowest?

This is the fun thing: the lowest score reveals how you are really feeling, and the other emotional dimensions are out of harmony with it. Therefore, you are really operating on all dimensions at this lowest point. Great if it is say, 78 per cent, but not if life is so hard for you at the moment and your score is 16 per cent.

If you have scored in the negative range, that is, below 50 per cent, then what is happening is that your emotional energy is stressed and well below where you should be – say operating between 50 per cent and 90 per cent. I often say that 100 per cent and 0 per cent are unachievable as you will be dead: at 100 per cent you are a saint and being beatified in heaven, and at 0 per cent you have committed suicide successfully and have ended all the pain.

Now the trick is to understand that we are not responsible for the hurts and slights we receive as we grow up. Our families, schools, workplaces may not have operated in our best interests to grow as an individual. Each blow that we receive puts us into more stress and shows in negative energy. Anger can be turned inwards against yourself, or it can be turned outwards to hurt others. Sadness can be realised as depression, and unto others as envy or greed. Finally, fear can be realised as anxiety, panic attacks and obsessive compulsions (to keep control of your environment) to being over-controlling of others. All these states are negative and are painful, but you may not recognise them as such, and that is why it is a good thing to try and measure what you are feeling at this moment in time.

We can conclude with the research that has been done, that Respectful Managers operate in the positive sides of the dimensions, which was demonstrated earlier with the CAT model and the virtues that go with it.

But what happens if you have received early trauma through no fault of your own, and yet are still stressed by it? I think the best thing to do is to receive some form of therapy. Counselling is always useful, and these days counsellors are able to offer different ways of dealing with the effects of trauma. Having these strategies lessens the impact and residual pain that we suffer and helps us overcome and slowly put ourselves into positive energy. It is my belief that it is these earlier traumas that lock us into stressed patterns of behaviour, but they need not determine your life forever. The first step is to shine the light of enlightenment so that you can understand that you are stressed and need help of some sort. These early traumas affect all areas of your life, it is not peculiar to the workplace. I know this as I have undertaken this on my own with some directional counselling and have achieved a positive-energy way of living and working.

I am convinced that Likeable Fraudsters, for instance, have been dreadfully harmed in their childhood, and when a similar stressful situation occurs again, the manager turns to fraud as the only solution that they can see to relieve their stress. Let me give you an example. Consider a well-functioning manager whom everyone likes and gets along with really well, who then starts to steal when their partner starts demanding to live the high life, with expensive clothes, houses and the like. All are out of reach for the manager. This triggers an earlier trauma, say sexual or physical abuse, which remains unresolved, and the manager is very likely to steal, as he or she cannot live up to the fact that they are not capable of meeting their partner's demands. As managers have to be clever to get to where they are in the first place, if they have access to financial systems in the organisation they will often begin to steal by taking a 'loan'. In almost all circumstances, they will take the money and gamble it to try and win back the loan as well as the required amount to satisfy their partner. This only results in more losses, although there may be lucky strikes now and then, and so they take out another 'loan' to repeat the same exercise. They never want to hurt the organisation, or their partner, but it always ends up in misery, and the fraudster manager gives up and hands herself over to the authorities. They often commit suicide, which indicates the depths of despair that they can sink to.

How to let go of past trauma and transgressions that lock us into stressed patterns

It is relatively easy to let go of past insults to your character, yet many of us find it one of the hardest things to do. In facing up to the past, you will see that your actions were compromised by these stressors and this is exactly how they come about. I do know how difficult it is to set down the path of reformation of what you truly should be without all those stresses in your life. It took me six months of work to get back to scratch and to find myself, who I truly am. I am an adoptee and it is now recognised that separation from one's mother in the first two years of life creates the deepest wound for anyone to recover from (Verrier, 1993). The problem is that the baby does not recognise that the mother as an independent being, so when mother disappears from her life, it feels like half of the baby has died. So, I can say with some authority on a sample of one, that to face up to one's wounds and heal oneself is possible and easy enough to do.

I say that it is easy, yes, if you are determined to reprogramme your life, but it is the hardest thing to do because we get locked into fear. As a wonderful all-knowing Buddhist monk told me, people see the dark room of their mind where all fears are locked into, as full of venomous snakes. But all you have to do is open the door and switch the light on and you will see old ropes lying on the floor (Gede Prama, 2018).This is a beautiful story that fits with myself and many – and I mean many – people whom I have had the privilege to meet and help with their changes. It does not happen in one miraculous moment but speedy gains can be made in within a year. There will be times that present opportunities for your brain to respond in the old ways, but if you can recognise the situation, which you will, you will have a choice to respond in the old or the new way. We do know about the plasticity of the brain, something we did not when I undertook my recovery. Now we have the science that backs mine and many others' claim that old habits can be changed, and quite swiftly at that.

One thing that you should know is that negative behaviour conceals from us the reality that we are less than perfect. It is that internal drive for perfection that is destructive of good patterns of behaviour. What must happen is that the individual has to recognise why and how they use negative behaviour in the first place. It is not a natural form of behaving; at heart we are communal and wish to live in harmony. To be so means that we cannot be destructive to others and harmful to ourselves.

That is the killer statement underlying this bad behaviour that we see all around us every day. People act as though they are totally unaware of the effect on others. Tyrant Managers ultimately lose control when they die. Almost all those in the workplace are allowed to leave, assuming they are not enslaved through debt to their employers. Mediocre Managers never last for long at the top and always fear that they will be toppled by the next wave of managers. Both these types must resent the Respectful Managers as they demonstrate the truth that you can be yourself in the workplace, and you know what? Co-workers actually prefer to work with Respectful rather than Malevolent types.

The strive to be the top dog with the most money and have the largest number of employees is a false pathway. The task for many in management is to reach to the highest position that they can attain. There is power and control at the top, whereas there is far less in the middle ranks of organisations. That is why Mediocres and Tyrants need those top positions, so they can control many people and larger budgets, and receive salaries and bonuses accordingly. That pathway to power, however, is not a happy one, especially if one has to lie and cheat and sabotage other managers to get there. To be truly happy at work means to operate at one's best, which is unachievable if most of your working time is spent competing against others. Management has not yet been promoted to an Olympic sport, yet so many Malevolent Managers do not realise this. To them, to come second is scorned.

However, as a Respectful Manager you can operate to the maximum that you can achieve. You manage your people respectfully, budgets are controlled and adhered to, performance of outputs is enhanced to the optimum. Brokering for your team is done without lies and taking credit for their work; it is a managerial activity that is done to ensure that co-workers get their fair share of resources. Good managers, i.e. Respectful ones, make sure that the details are attended to, so that upper management can be accurately informed; they also innovate with their co-workers in making processes more efficient.

How to choose a Respectful Manager for mentoring

You have to do your research carefully to find the right mentor for you. Many a mediocre manager will promote themselves as respectful when they are not. Talk to the manager's co-workers, see what they think. Ask around the management community if the manager has a good reputation or not. Remember, we are not looking for stellar performance, we do not need to, we are looking for a Respectful Manager who can bring out the best in you. Often the stars of business are not respectful at all; they may say the right things, but underneath it all, there is a Tyrant or Mediocre Manager.

How to approach a respectfully managed workplace for a job without harming your career

There are two factors to this section. One is that you may need to really rethink your career, and the other is to not let people know at work that you are looking for a different job. The latter is always a difficult task, especially if you work in a niche market or a geographically constrained one. For example, in the oil and gas industry, recruiters know every single top manager as there are not that many available, particularly with a shrinking labour force as the baby-boomers retire. A Respectful Manager will appreciate that you are still working and would not call up your boss for a reference. Malevolent Managers just do not care, so they will call your boss and spill the beans. It is imperative that you have evaluated your recruiter despite the enticements he or she may be offering. Other processes must take place first to be very sure that you are the right candidate for the position. Reference checking is usually the very last action of the recruitment process.

However, being in the wrong social class or having the wrong background makes some shudder at their job prospects; also if you are the 'wrong' gender, age, ethnicity, or have a disability. Nevertheless, it is still possible to find yourself another position. For example, a recent migration has taken place to Europe from the Syrian, Sudanese and Afghan wars, in which many have walked thousands of miles to seek refuge. Almost all the refugees want to live and work in peace, and pick up their lives from the devastation that the wars have imposed. I have no idea what it must feel like for those refugees, but I have made huge moves in my lifetime and each move has had its drawbacks;

it has found me in a different society despite the same language. Seeking a job can be the first time you experience racism – I was classified as a Pom in Australia, a derogatory term for the English. Imagine then that you cannot speak the language and have a different colour skin: your job prospects will be pretty low and almost zero, but may be better than where you come from. I think it is laughable to slur refugees as opportunists. Anyone who has lived in a warm climate has little or no desire to live in a cold one, particularly when the winter temperatures are below freezing.

All in all, it may be necessary for you to move to a workplace outside your comfort zone. For the last 8,000 years there has been a steady migration from rural environments to urban ones where there is perceived to be work. Most of us these days live in urban environments whether we like it or not. So, moving to another area may have to take place if you cannot find work in your own region. Video communications have become very useful in keeping in touch with people around the world and help anyone with a portable phone to be in touch with distant loved ones.

Another option is to make a sideways move that is not harmful to your career; you may need more patience to achieve your aims perhaps, but usually there will be new things to learn and other co-workers to get to know. Perhaps it may mean learning another language, but that is not so difficult as it first seems.

Upskilling is another way to beat Malevolent Management. Learning a new technique, skill or qualification is always a positive sign for recruiters and HR personnel, as it shows how willing you are to learn. They know that learners adapt more quickly into positions and that the settling in period will be shorter and less problematic. In each of these situations when it comes to contacting referees, which should be at the end of the recruitment process, you can forewarn your recruiter that the work that you are applying for is different for whatever reasons (and outline your prepared answer for this), so calling up your old manager is not very useful for the new job at hand.

Do not, under any circumstances, voluntarily quit your job. This job search must take place out of hours and on your own computer or device. To use your employer's time and resources is effectively stealing. You do not need to make such a mistake at the end of your employment; revenge is not sweet, it is wrongful.

My recommendation is that you must not vacate any position of your own accord until the next job is secured, but your manager may make life difficult for you as you work out your notice period, or even fire you on the spot – the tyrant's way of dealing with personnel issues. But this is all short-term pain for long-term gain, so take the punches and roll with them, as they will soon pass. I also tell my managers to not even give referee names until the last minute. Sometimes organisations have forms to fill in and demand referees before you even get to interview. Just stick to your guns and say that you will happily supply them when it becomes necessary. If you do not get an interview because of this, you have saved yourself from joining a malevolent organisation.

I also advise people to make judgements on the next workplace. Discernment is a wonderful thing, and you do not want to have it in hindsight only. My favourite is to visit the toilets on site; you can do this when you are being interviewed or being shown around the intended workplace. You may end up in a front office toilet, but check if it is clean. This is imperative, as it is the toilets in malevolently run organisations that people forget to clean or do not bother with. This is a factor on which you can make informed judgements. I do not mind if the toilet facilities are old. The point is, are they clean? I was quite amazed when visiting a glass factory that visitors were shown the toilets that the staff used, and the facilities were impeccably clean, with lots of soap, warm water and towels as well as air driers. This told me that the managers in this factory really cared about their workers – a good sign of respectful management.

It may seem a little trite to advise you to check out the toilets, but it is one of the best signs yet that I have seen of an organisation's true character. It also goes in line with the front office–back office routines that are a part of impression management. Forget how the website looks, it was probably made by others anyway, so check out smaller points of detail that management do have a say in. Clean walls are another factor. I am not looking for up to date paintwork, just walls and doors that are not grubby from consistent use. You know the type of dirt I mean: it takes years to accumulate around door handles and light switches and so on. The more back office you can get to see before an interview, the better. Remember that Malevolent Managers are inconsistent, even the fraudulent ones, although it may take you longer to recognise this.

There can be inconsistencies in preparing the stage for the factory floor, or even the waiting room. Check to see if Reception really are doing their job and receiving you correctly and with respect. Many doctors' or dentists' outer waiting areas are full of dog-eared old reading material: always a good sign that this medical practitioner is not up to date herself and does not really care about her patients. Check where the parking is and gauge how much better the car parking is for the managers as compared to the normal slots. I have seen plenty of car parks where I breathe a sigh of despair that management are allocated the best spots. Are they really so weak that such a walk as the others have to do is going to kill them? Of course not, but they see this as a management perk, which is really old-fashioned as the furthest parking spot is the healthiest one, as it forces you to walk further to the office every day and gives your heart a little bit of exercise.

9 How to develop Respectful Managers

In today's climate of job scarcity and malevolent forces at work with consumerism and status seeking, it is a little difficult to get the right managers in. It is bad enough with the self-promoting Mediocre Managers who will say or do anything to get the job at hand. Recruiting people is always difficult and expensive. But what if they had the right education? That would be certainly something to look out for. Maybe one day we will see adverts saying: 'Only Respectful Managers need apply'.

Training and development that really works

Education helps to provide the means to lead. Becoming a Respectful Manager is exactly that, self-realisation of hopes and ambitions to be the best that there can be. Anyone can be an atrocious manager. It takes guts, and strength of character to step out of that mould and become the best manager that can possibly be. To be led respectfully is precisely what I envisage and it is within the realms of possibility that anyone can change to become respectful, if not already showing promise in that area.

If you are not kept up to date in your business education, then complain. The educational institution is letting you down. Ask for your money back, the more requests that are made the better, it gives a feedback mechanism to their marketing that these institutions have to change. Learning about virtues is far more important than learning about Pareto optima and double entry ledgering.

When you think about it, correcting someone else's behaviour is fraught with difficulties, least of all as none of us likes to be corrected. There may be a few saints in organisations who thrive on corrections but not so with most of us. Using Non-Violent Communication (NVC) is an honourable way of being able to put forward real concerns by opposing parties. In my view, managers should be trained immediately in NVC before appointment to any supervisory position. The process cannot be manipulated and it cannot be used to have power over people. It recognises that all parties need to have their needs met, no matter how different and contradictory those needs may be. People who are involved in the NVC process often remark that they never thought it could work. Now, it is used in many areas of the world, but I never see it employed in organisations. This is partly because businesses are not interested in NVC, they prefer to outmanoeuvre the other side. The millions of battles that take place in our courts point to how unsatisfactory the legal forum is, with lawyers trying to outdo each other with case precedents and clever arguments. This is not based on needs of each party! This is based on an industry that has grown as it recognised that big fees could be gained by advocacy and pushing forward legal arguments. It is often said, put two lawyers in the same room and within minutes they will start arguing. This does not happen with NVC, and the reason is that the process is based on respect. If we could harness the talents of young lawyers away from commercial law and into NVC negotiation we would have the world of workplaces in much better shape. Issues become defused, parties realise that the old way of thinking was getting them nowhere, and with resolutions that are always mutually agreeable, peace can reign.

There are of course mediation counsellors, but there is one thing missing from this industry and that is that the parties are not obligated to do what they said that they would do. Arbitration is a process that binds two parties no matter how the parties feel or want to have that particular resolution. So why not use NVC within the workplace? I suspect that a Respectful Manager has learnt to use an NVC process via years of experience; however, it is also incumbent on those who work under him to do so. You can only deal with hostilities from the accounts department with operations if you have a legitimate power over them, so it puts resolution into the lap of the CEO. The many CEOs that I have met often do not take this opportunity and leave squabbles to be sorted out among the lower ranks; they see their role as CEO is to look after strategy. That is why I think any manager who is being educated must do a stint of learning and practising NVC. Malevolent Managers, particularly the Mediocre type which forms the largest segment of managers, can be retrained if they want to be. It requires tremendous motivation on the individual's part to do so, but it is possible. With that in mind, here is what I consider the right education to make Respectful Managers.

There is much written on management education, but it cannot be correct as our organisations are infested with Malevolent Managers. Business schools have made management education a big industry with the likes of Harvard (USA), London Business School (UK) and INSEAD (France) being the three leaders. So how can we effectively develop co-workers into Respectful Managers? I think that the best way is to educate them about values and ethics first, using the virtues as the foundation. It has already been found that when used in families, schools and communities the virtues make real changes in people's behaviour and their awareness of their effect on others.

Business students must learn how to use Non-Violent Communication (Rosenberg, 1998). It has worked in troubled hotspots in the world, like Palestine and Israel and for hostage negotiations and so forth. This is not an optional unit, it is imperative that all management students learn how to listen to the other party and develop reasonable solutions for both. NVC is not a manipulation tool, it is authentic listening to the other person's needs and wants. The two parties have to be present in the sense of presenting their real needs to be exposed. For example: a person demands higher wages, the manager has a tight budget and it is impossible. The two parties then give their needs, one needs more money, the other needs no breaking of the budget. Then as they work through their needs, they can explore possibilities: perhaps re-training the co-worker, or promotion to a higher paid position when the time comes. In this example, the parties can reach agreement, but it relies on both being honest in stating their needs. The reader may see already that it will change a Malevolent Manager who is only focussed on his or her own needs, if they understand that it is only through helping others that their ambitions can be fulfilled. NVC is already taught in classrooms and needs practice to become at ease with the process and consolidate. When this methodology is internalised, there is a turnaround of a Malevolent Manager into a Respectful one. But say we have a highly manipulative manager who is very clever at using such processes to his advantage?

We know that co-workers know a Respectful Manager when they see one, so the best way is to have a practicum to assess how well the virtues and NVC are embedded. We know that it is impossible for Malevolent Managers to keep up their disguises when working alongside co-workers. So why not provide a qualification coupled with practicum(s), to indicate that the person has reached such a level? It is easy enough to do, and the 360-degree evaluations of fellow co-workers during the practicum would prove whether or not that the person has achieved the desired behaviour.

There is a pool of co-workers that always want to become managers, so it is time that we put in place a vocational qualification for them to become supervisors, and they later graduate with the degree or diploma of Respectful Management. We allow pharmacists to practise their arts on a public that is aware that the person may be a trainee and that the practice is being monitored. Very few people would say that they do not want a trainee to assist them, and so it would be the same with co-workers. The practicum would have to be at least one year in duration, and preferably another shorter one at the beginning of the period of study to acquaint the individual with managerial practice. This qualification can be easily funded by large organisations or governments that need Respectful Management, and they can assist other organisations in developing a pool of practitioners.

If this is done, we will find a surge of managers who will be diverse in culture, gender, age, disability and race. Thus, in less than one generation, we will change the face of management completely. So, who is big enough to take on the challenge? Will it be the software and telecoms organisations? Financial institutions and banks? Governments? The organisations with the biggest risks of bad management should be the ones to stand up and contribute to this new format of managerial education. After all, they will benefit the most, as will their shareholders.

Respect can be instituted by example from the top

What about turning around managers who are already in situ in an organisation? The best way I have found is to use shadowing. The party concerned does not like to be shadowed at best, and at worst will sabotage the correcting methodology all the way through. However, shadowing is the only way to reform such Malevolent Managers if, and only if, the shadower has the legitimate power to do so. If the party realises that his job is at stake, then that may be enough to halt poor performance and institute change.

The exercise is costly, effectively using two managers to do one person's job, but direct coaching in place at work is often the only way that a manager can see what he is doing is disrespectful, and that to gain the respect of co-workers one has to be respectful. Every single task, whether it is writing an email, correcting a co-worker's performance, work meeting and so forth, has to be shadowed carefully. Think if you like of a guardian angel by the manager's side. An angel would be fair, thoughtful and kind in delivering feedback, as well as encouraging positive behaviour. Many people would fear such an exercise, but it is the only way of getting to the foundations of the behaviour. This will inevitably be low self-worth, envy or greed and anxiety, if you remember the CAT model of earlier.

It may seem to be a social stigma in the organisation for a manager to receive such obvious direct help, but it is effective and may only need to take a month or so. We know that it takes a few weeks for a habit to be changed (Lally et al., 2011); once ingrained with the manager concerned there has to be demonstration of this and when this fails and the manager falls into the old ways, a word in the ear will help to keep that individual on the pathway to change. Again, new neural pathways are formed and the old ones become less and less used. At last, we social agents have science on our side; the sense making of shadowing is more likely to be taken up by senior management.

The stigma has to be addressed, and what I suggest is that the manager wears a badge or sticker which is an 'L plate' to indicate that we are still learning. The L plate is universal thanks to uniform driving regulations throughout the world; a country may have a different word, but everyone recognises it as a learner driver. Here in France it is the letter A, Hungary has a T plate, the Japanese have a *shoshinsha* mark, and so on. If the CEO is the first one to wear this badge, and publicly undergoes some retraining herself, or more likely, reinforcement of positive behaviour, then others will accept it much more willingly. The learner badge has to be worn at all times, even outside when on business. The kudos of wearing such a badge would be overwhelming: it says to the world that the wearer is a life-long learner. A certificate will be issued to the graduate of the learner badge, when and only when the guardian angel supervisor gives the authority to do so, and then a small badge with a check mark is worn. The wearing of the badges alerts others in the workplace that malevolent behaviour will not be tolerated and that the wearer's own behaviour is under constant scrutiny by their co-workers. The

Malevolent Managers who are not willing to undergo such a lengthy inspection would be the only ones fearful of such an exercise and will find excuses to leave, and so the energy in the organisation is changed where before it was negative, and positive behaviours are reinforced. It always has to start at the top as the power changes to legitimate and not the lesser forms of power that we see exercised by Malevolent Managers.

My firm of Guardian Angels was set up to provide locums for small business owners to cover them while they are away. Few small business owners could trust an outsider to operate their businesses in their absence so not many could take up the service. But a better way of using trusted managers is to use them in a shadow program. These Guardian Angel managers would have undergone specific training and education, so that organisations would be assured that the shadow program is effective. All work is grounded on positive energy and the virtues in our behaviour in the workplace.

This idea is not new under the sun. In ancient Greece there was a culture of mentoring that covered far more areas than just politics and business; in Japan there are virtuous circles, which they learnt is the most effective way of getting nations out of poverty; and with the Bali Mula, they set up their village councils in a circle with each member having a double on the other side of the circle so that they learn together at their appropriate level and there is not one village chief, but two.

Management team exercises using real trust instead of games

In a positive energy organisation, management team exercises must use genuine trust instead of games. One such example is the management team exercise that I have set up in Bali, so that the executive team come to grips with trust and respect at deeper levels, and build new roofs for impoverished people. The thing is that they have to work alongside the family and friends who come to help. They will learn about respect and the service values of the Balinese in a five-day build. The team exercise manager is on site and allows information to be passed to either party. This way there is instant feedback on behaviour in their relationships with each other and the family. This exercise is restricted to only five members as the numbers are critical to allow social relationships to be developed. There are other service-type team exercises that can be found in other countries, so a good trawl on the internet should be done. Whichever team exercise is undertaken, the bottom line is to encourage trust among the management team. Without this, the organisation is doomed to malevolent behaviour, disorganisation, petty empire building and silos. Not great for the organisation and its shareholders, and even worse for the co-workers.

10 Moving organisations forward to being Respectful workplaces

Change to good management?

The first step for change is to measure what is already in existence inside the organisation. Co-workers will be interviewed to assess which managers are Malevolent and which are Respectful. This can be done via a survey and only takes 15 minutes. The proviso to this is that the survey has to remain independent and without reprisals to the respondents. If this is guaranteed by management, then this information can be analysed using the Executive Impression Management typology for the first measurement. I would suggest this is done 6-monthly but can be done sooner if transformational change is imperative. Co-workers will be astonished to see that their frank answers will be publicly available but not in any identifiable format, as usually this information sinks without trace. These quanta of information should not be used in any competitive way, otherwise this is fuel for Malevolent Managers to start their politicking, which is a waste of everyone's time and energy.

The next step is to offer a change program to all of the individual managers, even those who are respectful; this sets the tone of the organisation as people are able to see that something concrete is being done with their own manager, good, bad or indifferent. This training is done using the virtues as the foundation. Virtues are common knowledge so Malevolent Managers can easily talk the talk but we know now that they cannot consistently walk the walk, so they will expose themselves very quickly to their co-workers.

When I say co-workers, I mean subordinates as well as colleagues and senior managers. The classic profile of a Mediocre Manager is that senior management may be impressed by the constant self-promotion that they engage in, and therefore see only their good points. However, subordinates will see different behaviour and this will offset the politics that are bound to happen.

Once measurement is completed, Malevolent Managers will be offered the Shadowing programme to change their behaviour in the workplace. I would aim for the highest-level managers first as there are more gains to be had, with immediate impact on co-workers. The quicker the upper hierarchy engage, the quicker the organisation undergoes massive change, almost automatically. But it is only the virtues that are emphasised in the first round. The Executive Impression Management theory is used for analysis.

No one is sacked or fired. Dismissals will only occur when there is documented intransigence over say, 6 months. I personally do not like dismissals as it so quickly brings legal advocacy which is more based on he with the largest pay-check wins. I find that the NVC process allows the Malevolent Manager's needs to be respectfully heard and that starts a dialogue of change. If he or she is unwilling to change then other career choices can be made and various programmes can be offered to that manager, for instance defining career options within and outside the organisation, an assisted job search, or even educational development.

Thankfully we know from the CAT model that positive and negative energies can never unite so when the Malevolent Managers read the writing on the wall, they will all leave within 24 months of the first survey. One side effect that I have noticed is that some Respectful Managers may leave as well. This can be for a number of reasons, now that they see that the organisation is changing for the better. They may seek self-development and further study, retiring and smelling the roses, consulting work or even voluntary work. This fact sets upper management in a tailspin as they do not want to lose their good managers, but this will only result in a few leaving, not all. The sooner a training programme is set in place for promotion to management from subordinate co-workers the better.

Be aware though, co-workers may probably be tired of workplace change rhetoric, which is why the steps have to be put in place quickly and effectively. They will be surprised that anyone wants to listen to them, and once they have given their responses to the questionnaire, then they will want to see action. Massive turnarounds can be achieved within 6 months if all parties are willing and able to put in place the elements of virtues in their workplace. In this way, the discourse will match the actions. This results in less emotional violence in the workplace, including physical abuse and sexual innuendo. There is also a reduction in conflict. Silos can drop their walls, and even unions can see that their workers are being protected and no harm will come to them, malevolent or not. Different departments start speaking to each other and there will be a focus on the end-customer, raising efficiencies without overworking or overtime levels going through the roof.

In fact, what happens with the positive energy being raised is that harmony returns, or if it's the first time for the organisation, harmony is put in place and co-workers will be wanting to come to work rather than be absent from it. Co-workers will act as the check and balance to this energy by recognising bad behaviour quickly, and should be able to report this via an independent hotline with no reprisals. If hotlines are the number one tool to reduce managerial fraud, then think how effective it would be for reports of negative behaviour that threaten the harmony of the organisation. All reports need to be impartially and independently investigated. To stop needless or even malevolent reporting, put in place a rule that all hotline users must be able to provide evidence for their allegations. Sherron Watkins, the famous whistleblower at Enron, ensured that she had the financial sheets ready to be investigated. Requiring evidence keeps out the gossips and those with an axe to grind via the hotline. In this manner, the organisation has the best chance of change, with the Malevolent Managers leaving or being changed in their daily habits of using the organisation for their own ends.

11 Conclusion

I would like to wrap up this book with the rather bold statement that the theory that I stumbled across, Executive Impression Management, works. It is so powerful that it can be used to detect fraudster managers who up until now mostly eluded the police and in-house investigation departments or internal auditors. It came about as I was trying to answer the question: who can I trust? And the answer is the Respectful Managers. They are consistent in their impression management and they never use the legitimate power invested in them by their status for their own ends. All co-workers can spot the Respectful Managers when they sound them out on these two criteria alone. The difficulty is that Malevolent Managers, particularly the fraudsters and the mediocre ones, will assume the guise of a Respectful Manager. However, the mask has cracks in it which others see, but shrug off the implications. I for one would never put a manager in place who uses deceit in any form, from tweaking their CVs for additional credit to deceiving large departments to work for them rather than the organisation's customers and investors. Deceivers are liars, and liars cheat. They cheat us, the general public, in many ways, through higher prices than are necessary, the red tape in our regulations, the oligarchies and cartels that are formed, pollution of our environment that we need to live and breathe in safely, and the end customer receives shoddy goods or services. Large populations are exploited, with low wages to ensure profits remain higher than they ought to be. When the workers in that country realise that they are exploited, the business moves the factory to another emerging nation that will work for low wages, and so the cycle continues.

I can say categorically that no Respectful Manager is behind such actions. All they want is harmony in their workplace so that their co-workers will receive the best care and attention and concomitant resources. By letting them run organisations we will see gains in all of the above areas. Co-workers are not confined to their work 24/7, they influence their peers, their families, their governments, and we should see a massive change. But I am not writing this specifically for that end, I am writing this book as I know from first-hand experience, social reports and operating a business where trust is the ultimate virtue, that most workplaces are demeaning and based on conflict, which in turn is wasteful and polluting our environment. Each abusive act committed by these Malevolent Managers hurts not only a co-worker, but their families and their children. Unfortunately, my children already operate in a malevolent world of management, but there is absolutely no need for my grandchildren to suffer the abuse and violence that exists in most workplaces today.

It cuts through the office politics of who likes who, that goes on through the ranks of organisations. Executive Impression Management gives us a code-breaking mechanism to cut through the constant white noise of Malevolent Managers. For the first time, we can expose who is who and uncover the real giants in the workplace – the Respectful Managers.

The emergence of Respectful Manager Executive Impression Management has been a fortunate finding to help us all. Never before have power and consistency been considered as the two major factors in the workplace. We now know what the Respectful Manager looks and behaves like. They are clearly recognisable. Co-workers will not be deceived once they have read this book, and if you only pass this on to one more person, the act of changing these awful workplaces begins. With such knowledge, we will not be deceived by Malevolent Managers ever again. Their tricks and deceptions are exposed here so that you can see them for what they are, selfish people who use organisations for their own needs for power and control.

Attendant on that, we have a new model to train and develop respectful workers to become managers, using the foundations of what makes a manager respectful. Their good behaviour must be rewarded accordingly, not pushed aside in games of organisational politics. The water cooler can be a focus for encouragement and peace and not for promoting the chit-chat of others wanting their own power game.

This theory has given us, for the first time, a way that we can really change organisations and move forward to being respectful, by filling them up with their quota of Respectful Managers.

Our present workplaces can now have a peaceful, non-violent revolution with the proliferation of Respectful Managers, which is what this book espouses. It is now up to you, the reader, to evaluate what you have read and to take the theory to its application in the workplace. That way our efforts are rewarded bit by bit, forever. Good Management? We now have the answer, now let's do it.

References

Association of Certified Fraud Examiners (2018). *Report to the Nations 2018*. Austin, TX: Association of Certified Fraud Examiners, 79.

Avolio, B. J. and B. M. Bass (1999). 'Re-examining the components of transformational and transactional leadership using the Multifactor Leadership Questionnaire'. *Journal of Occupational and Organizational Psychology* 72(4): 441–462.

Bass, B. M., B. J. Avolio and L. Goodman (1987). 'Biography and the assessment of transformational leadership at the world-class level'. *Journal of Management* 13(1).

Baumeister, R. F., E. Bratslavsky, C. Finkenauer and K. Vohs (2001). 'Bad is stronger than good'. *Review of General Psychology* 5(4): 323–370.

Brotman, D. J., S. H. Golden and I. S. Wittstein (2007). 'The cardiovascular toll of stress'. *The Lancet* 370(9592): 1089 1100.

Calhoun, G. M. (1924). 'The jurisprudence of the Greek city'. *Columbia Law Review* 24(2): 154–171.

Doidge, N. (2007). *The Brain That Changes Itself: Stories of Personal Triumph from the Frontiers of Brain Science*. New York: Viking Press.

Einarsen, S. (1999). 'The nature and causes of bullying at work'. *International Journal of Manpower* 20(1–2): 16–28.

Faria, M. A. (2015). 'Neolithic trepanation decoded – A unifying hypothesis: Has the mystery as to why primitive surgeons performed cranial surgery been solved?' *Surgical Neurology International* 6(72).

Frankl, V. (2008). *Recollections: An Autobiography*. New York: Basic Books.

French, J. R. P. and B. H. Raven (1960). 'The bases of social power'. In D. Cartwright and A. Zander (eds) *Group Dynamics: Research and Theory*. Evanston, IL: Harper and Row, 607–623.

Goffman, E. (1959). *The Presentation of Self in Everyday Life*. New York: Anchor Books, Doubleday.

Goffman, E. (1967). *Interaction Ritual: Essays on Face-to-Face Behavior*. New York: Pantheon Books.

Hendrikse, G. (2003). *Economics and Management of Organizations: Co-ordination, Motivation and Strategy*. New York: McGraw-Hill.

Keynes, J. M. (2007). *General Theory of Employment, Interest and Money*. New Delhi: Atlantic Publishers & Distributors.

Kramer, S. N. (1963). *The Sumerians: Their History, Culture and Character*. Chicago: University of Chicago Press.

Lally, P., J. Wardle and B. Gardner (2011). 'Experiences of habit formation: A qualitative study'. *Psychology, Health and Medicine* 16(4): 484–489.

Machiavelli, N. (1532). *The Prince*. Italy: Antonio Blado d'Asola.

Marmot, M. G., G. Rose, M. Shipley and P. J. Hamilton (1978). 'Employment grade
and coronary heart disease in British civil servants'. *Journal of Epidemiology and
Community Health* 32(4): 244–249.

Myers, I. B. with P. B. Myers (1995). *Gifts Differing: Understanding Personality Type*.
Mountain View, CA: Davies-Black.

Oswald, A. J., E. Proto and D. Sgroi (2015). 'Happiness and productivity'. *Journal of
Labor Economics* 33(4): 789–822.

Peter, L. J. (1969). *The Peter Principle*. New York: William Morrow.

Prama, G. (2018). 'Bell of peace'. Retrieved 14 May 2018, from https://www.bellofpea
ce.org/

Press Association (2015). 'Social media domestic abusers face up to five years in jail'.
29 December.

Quinn, R. E. (1988). *Beyond Rational Management*. San Francisco: Jossey-Bass.

Reeves, K. (2000). 'Racism and projection of the shadow'. *Psychotherapy: Theory,
Research, Practice, Training* 37(1): 80–88.

Rosenberg, M. (1998). *Nonviolent Communication: A Language of Life*. Echinitas, CA:
Puddle Dancer Press.

Samaritans https://www.samaritans.org/news/ONS-suicide-statistics. Accessed 13 May
2018.

Seligman, M. (1998). *Learned Optimism: How to Change Your Mind and Your Life*.
New York: Pocket Books.

Sheridan, T. A. (2005). *Voicing Women Managers' Unemployment Experience in Australia: The Hidden Toll*. Perth, WA: Women Chiefs of Enterprises International, 1–100.

Sheridan, T. A. (2014). *Managerial Fraud*. Farnham, Surrey: Gower.

Sheridan, T. A. (2016). *Malevolent Managers*. Farnham, Surrey: Gower.

Sutton, R. I. (2010). *Good Boss, Bad Boss: How to Be the best … and Learn from the
Worst*. New York: Business Plus.

Taylor, F. W. (1911). *The Principles of Scientific Management*. New York: Harper and
Row.

Verrier, N. N. (1993). *The Primal Wound: Understanding the Adopted Child*. Louisville,
KY: Gateway Press.

Virtues Project International Association (1991). 'The Virtues Project'. Retrieved 14
April 2016, from https://www.virtuesproject.com/

Watkins, S. and J. L. Pearce (2003). 'Former Enron vice president Sherron Watkins on
the Enron collapse: Address to the Academy'. *Academy of Management Executives*
17(4): 119–125.

Index

Page numbers in bold and italics refer to information in tables and figures respectively.